The Rediscovery

of Inner Experience

Lucy Bregman

The Rediscovery
of Inner Experience

Nelson-Hall nh Chicago

LIBRARY OF CONGRESS CATALOGING IN PUBLICATION DATA

Bregman, Lucy
  The rediscovery of inner experience.

  Bibliography: p.
  Includes index.
  1. Experience (Religion) 2. Experience.
3. Psychology, Religious. I. Title.
BL53.B66   291.4'2   81–22600
ISBN 0–88229–686–8   AACR2

Manufactured in the United States of America

10 9 8 7 6 5 4 3 2 1

The paper in this book is pH neutral (acid-free).

Contents

In this book about inner experiences and their rediscovery by contemporary psychology, we have chosen to attempt several things. First, we will introduce readers to psychological literature on six inner experiences: dreams, daydreams, mystical states, madness, orgasm, and dying. However different these experiences may be, all have been seen as vitally important due to their capacity to reveal the authentic nature of persons and ultimate reality. Second, we will examine the beliefs and background assumptions of the contemporary popular literature, beliefs which help account for the enthusiastic stance toward inner experiences. We will use the term "inner experience advocates" when referring to those who hold this set of beliefs. Third, we will offer a description of "psychological religiousness" as it emerges from the writings of inner experience advocates, and examine the way in which it functions in the context of contemporary American social and religious structures.

The phrase "psychological religiousness" may come as a surprise to some readers, used perhaps to a Freudian opposition between religion and psychology. In the writings on inner experience, however, psychology is no longer the enemy of true religion; but as we will demonstrate, it has become the vehicle for a new form of religiousness, a new way to encounter sacrality and ultimacy. The foci of this new religiousness will emerge gradually throughout our presentation of the material on the six experiences.

The inner experience materials range from the learned to the popular, and from the profound and really worthwhile to the utterly trashy. We have tried to include both ends of each continuum. One reason for this is to give the reader a sense that interest in inner experience is a popular phenomenon, boasting a large number of how-to-do-it, self-help books on various relevant topics. Another set of documents are autobiographies; we will turn to these especially when discussing madness. Other works are more scholarly, academic presentations by psychologists; even these are sometimes unabashed in their advocacy of particular experiences. Never in what follows do we wish to equate popular with trashy, and, in fact, some of the general audience works are a great deal more sensitive and complex in their portraits of human existence than are the more academic theoretical ones. Readers surely have their own ideas as to what constitutes trash, but our criteria relate to oversimplification of life's dilemmas, and the reliance on magical formulas for success—two themes that appear frequently throughout inner experience writings.

Throughout the literature we will examine, the very word *experience* has a polemical connotation. Rather than provide a once-and-for-all definition of the term, we will show how it has been used to express a certain standard of authenticity and courageousness. At its core, this also connotes a religious reality, an encounter with an Ultimate or a source of value which can give meaning and fullness to life. By revealing some of the religious connotations of the term experience (rather than belaboring its exact philosophical meanings) the stage will be set for examining the six inner experiences rediscovered and rehabilitated by contemporary psychological writers.

Will this book advocate "inner experience advocacy"? Will we encourage and advance the cause of psychological religiousness? To devote an entire book to a subject is to judge it worthy of attention, to take seriously a phenomenon which has often been brushed aside as trivial or condemned out of hand as worthless. However, as the reader will see, our attention is far from an unqualified endorsement, and our efforts will include a serious critique of the beliefs, values and assumptions of inner experience advocates. As a scholar of religion, one is asked to take all forms of religion seriously, including those forms which one can neither accept for oneself nor recommend to others. This principle is built into the method of scholarly religious studies whether the object of study be the most worthy religiousness of the saints, or the Aztec rituals of human sacrifice. Surely nontraditional materials which contain the seeds of a new religious ethos ought to receive the same methodological respect. We hope that with such a stance, uncritical opponents of psychological religiousness may prepare themselves to see some of its strengths and its appeal, while uncritical advocates may begin to question the adequacy of its assumptions about persons, society, and the nature of existence. Just as this author has shifted her own opinions and convictions since beginning this study, so too readers may find themselves drawn into new perspectives, and forced to leave behind dearly-held illusions. Our conviction is that the discomfort this may cause is much less than the price one must pay for clinging blindly and narrowly to any particular set of beliefs and attitudes, including a dogmatic spirit of moral and religious relativism.

The World
of Inner Experience

What is an experience? For us, William James provides the key to the meaning of experience. He defends the authority of the Bible on the grounds that it contains "a true record of the inner experiences of great-souled persons wrestling with the crises of their fate."[1] Then he contrasts two types of religious life. To the ordinary person,

> religion has been made for him by others, communicated to him by tradition, determined to fixed forms by imitation and retained by habit. It would profit us little to study this second hand religious life. We must make search rather for the original experiences which were the pattern-setters to all this mass of suggested feeling and imitated conduct. These experiences we can find only in individuals for whom religion exists not as a dull habit, but as an acute fever rather.[2]

The crucial contrast is between tradition and inner experience, between secondhand and firsthand religion, between what is inherited and thus socially given and what is authentically the individual's own immediate reality. Most of the inner experience literature rests upon this dichotomy. A champion of liberated sexuality repeats James' contrast by claiming "If culture programs us through words, direct experience transcends words."[3] Again and again, the dichotomy reappears often in contrast with intellectual reflection upon experience:

> Some of you are probably thinking, but what about the *meaning* of dreams, the *symbolism* of dreams? You want to *understand.* In gestalt therapy, we don't worry about understanding, we concentrate on *experience.* [4]

Here, conceptual knowledge and language itself are assimilated into the "socially given" category, while direct experience is freed from all contamination from culturally bound conceptual frameworks. What for James were two kinds of religion become two ways of living in the world: one immediate, firsthand, and free from the confines of society and the past, the other dominated by "dull habit" and reliance on others' judgments. "Experience" is thus a moral category, to a degree hard to overestimate.

But what about "an experience," a usage current throughout the literature? What does it mean to have one and how can one tell if one has experienced or not? "If you doubt whether or not you've had an orgasm, then you haven't": this piece of folk wisdom stands as one answer to such queries. An "experience" is immediately self-authenticating, at least for many writers. However, in the case of certain types of experiences, such as mystical states, the possibility is allowed that a person might have the experience, know that something special has happened, and yet neither know nor care that the proper label for what was experienced was "mystical state of consciousness." In other words, what is really beyond our doubt is the fact that something out of the ordinary happened, something memorable and personally significant. Although it might be possible to mislabel an experience (which is why the truism about orgasms is in fact untrue), it is not possible to overlook the occurrence of something without resorting to repression or self-deception.

In the literature on inner experience, the beyond-all-doubt nature of having experienced something combines with the moral imperative to trust one's own experiences rather than be guided by tradition. Since the possibility of an honest mistake ("I thought I experienced something, but I guess I didn't") is eliminated, the key question is: Shall I remain true to my own experience or repress it? To repress it requires, in this context, an act of semi-intentional forgetting, ignoring or denying, for the sake of clinging to socially derived models of what ought to be the case. Because inner experience advocates insist that we take responsibility for our experiences, repression is in principle avoidable—a very different understanding than Freud's. Curiously, in the inner experience literature itself, we will again and again confront cases which undermine this rather simplistic view. People in dream studies swore they were tossing and turning with insomnia, but the electroencephalogram (EEG) showed they had been sleeping soundly. People under the influence of LSD swore they had religious experiences although researchers thought that some (admittedly unusual) sensory distortions were being beefed up by words like *sacred* and *mystical.* And several generations of women, steeped in Freudian theory, dutifully reported two kinds of orgasm—vaginal and clitoral. In short, honest mistakes are possible —or perhaps, the desire to report certain experiences will itself generate a kind of self-deception.

According to the dominant view, then, to have an experience leads directly to a moral and religious decision: should one attend to the experience, rely on it and defend

its validity, or should one flee back toward the safety of
"secondhand" living? Even the reliance on other "great-
souled" persons' experiences would be a mistake, so that
the lesson to be learned from the religious geniuses of the
past is not imitation but a resolute pursuit of one's own
experiencing. Sixty years after James, Abraham Maslow
repeated this argument in a form which became extraordinarily persuasive for the current generation of inner
experience advocates. The value of tradition, according to
Maslow, is that it has no value, but in most cases acts as
a barrier to cultivating and taking seriously one's own
awareness.

Another way to express the moral and personal meanings surrounding the term experience is to imagine an
individual experiencer placing a plaque at a certain locale: "On this spot, on the sixteenth day of March, 1977, Joe
Doe had a mystical experience." Or, "On this spot, the
night of May 8, 1972, Jane Doe experienced a lucid
dream." The purpose of such a plaque would be to mark
off, to commemorate, an important or unique happening
in the life of the experiencer. It would also be a kind of
public testimony to the power of certain experiences to
affect those who live through them. The inner experience
literature is filled with such testimonies. Such a marker is
also a way to insist that the experience involved is transformative; Joe Doe looks back on March 16, 1977, and
forever after will be able to say, "That was when I became
who I am now" or "That was when I learned to rely on my
own firsthand religiousness rather than someone else's
tradition." The appropriateness of this symbol of the
plaque derives from one's certainty of having experienced; it would be no good at all to commemorate
something one only believed to have happened.

If direct experience is always morally superior to both
tradition and socially given concepts, there can never be
a problem of too much experience, of too many plaques. In
fact, collecting experiences for their own sake might be

morally desirable, as a method of liberating oneself systematically from the dead hand of tradition. Without question, the self-actualized person's "basic philosophy is to experience and learn as much as possible,"[5] an idea pervasive in the literature. Or, as one of many "Guidelines to Avoid Sexual Hangups": "List your sexual aversions and those acts you've never tried. Then see if you might not attempt each one, at least in fantasy."[6] At this level, the inner experience literature duplicates the ethos of consumer culture, in which the injunction to "Try something new and different" becomes a moral imperative (and a commercially valuable one). As we shall see, the moral dilemma of too much experience is disallowed, as are the possible negative psychological consequences of the exhausting quest for more and more dreams, orgasms, or mystical states.

Critics often denounce this ethic of constant firsthand experiencing as "the search for kicks." Inner experience advocates try to avoid this charge by placing the quest for experiences in a broader moral and spiritual framework. Since kicks implies selfish, short-term pleasure, many inner experience writers would distinguish this shoddy kind of existence from a more authentic and courageous commitment to ultimate reality as revealed through one's own experiencing. Other inner experience writers claim that even the quest for selfish, short-term pleasure has a certain validity, and to deny this is to advocate the Puritan Ethic and the repressive aspects of Western religious tradition. Defenders of fantasy and sexual experiencing rely on this argument.

In looking at the meaning of experience, we have not yet explored the adjective *inner,* although this was part of James' original statement. Inner experiences are the topic of this book, and religion. But inner in what sense? Private? Yes—until these experiences become transformed (either verbally or in writing) into public testimony that "I had the experience." Inner in the sense of "within my skin?" Not quite. For among most of the authors writing on inner experiences, there is an awareness (however dimly expressed) that experiences do not have a physical location in quite the same way that tables, chairs, and parts of the body do. It is true that a plaque requires a physical location, but many writers suggest that "within one's head" is not the appropriate way to visualize the place of experiencing. Consciousness is not within one's head, although the brain, which most of us believe to be a prerequisite for consciousness, may be firmly localized within the skull.

In the context of experience, the adjective *inner* has a meaning. It implies an experience of inwardness, withinness, which may in fact destroy my ordinary notion of myself as a spectator locked within my own skin. "Withinness" is a symbolic category rather than a physical location. One favorite symbolic model of contemporary writers is the self as a series of concentric circles:

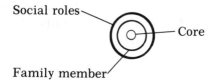

Internal to the self are personal roles such as mother, friend, lover. According to many of our authors, though these are more fundamental to ordinary ideas of identity, they are not authentically central to the self. One therapeutic instance of the image of self has the person moving "within":

The subject is asked to imagine his personality as though it were a series of concentric circles and to visualize the various layers in turn, starting with the outermost and proceeding toward the center or inner-

most core of her being. On the "outer" layers, a subject will usually encounter images expressing his
conflicts and defenses on the personality level,
whereas the "inner" layers contain the images of the
supraconsciousness and the transpersonal self, typically ending with an experience of intense universal
love or merging in light or with the sun.[7]

Although not all the writers share the vocabulary or
psychological presuppositions of this therapist, the symbol of multiple layers circling and enfolding a core is
popular.

What this suggests is that the meaning of inner is essentially symbolic. Journeys inward are a means to discover
a whole new realm. The explorers of this realm were
dubbed "astronauts of inner space" by some. Other specific symbols for experiencing inwardness would include
entering a cave, or diving to the depths of the sea. Even
where such visual motifs do not appear directly, there is
an implicit acknowledgment of such symbolism through
the often repeated promise of hidden inner potential bu-
ried within the self. At its most literalized, withinness
becomes equated with hidden body parts, and so "your
sexual response is locked within your own body." But even
here, the moral dimension overreaches the literal, so that
the author continues, "Just as you taste and digest your
own food, so you must take responsibility for your own
orgasm."[8] "Within" is ultimately a spiritual and moral
realm, and only on occasion a biological location.

As many contemporary writers are quick to point out,
this symbolic inwardness is by no means a recent discovery. Throughout religious history, both Eastern and Western, it has been employed lavishly to suggest the same
transition from a spiritual state of ordinary, externally
oriented consciousness to something different and higher.
The journey inward might take many forms, and need not
have the sophistication of, for example, St. Teresa's clas-

sic, *The Interior Castle*. But what unites inner experience advocates is a conviction that they are rediscovering an inner realm rather than creating it. Most of them see recent Western society as exceptional in its forgetfulness and neglect of this realm; even technologically primitive cultures knew inwardness and were at home with its landscape, whereas for most Americans today it is terra incognita. Because of the inherent richness of the symbolism of "inwardness," we feel that to label the experiences of dreaming, etc., as merely private is to lose something vital —as inner experience advocates would themselves insist.

Since no set of beliefs, moral attitudes or symbols appears full-blown without antecedents, it is worth asking for the antecedents of the Jamesian dichotomy between experience and tradition, and the moral imperative it contains. Are the beliefs about direct experience and its repression as self-evident as their exponents seem to feel? We think not. From an alternative perspective, all of us are enmeshed in tradition, and all our experiences—however direct, fulfilling, and authentically ours—are shaped by our social and religious heritage. Even those great-souled founders of religious traditions began within the traditions which had formed their lives and thoughts. The hope of experiencing anything outside all tradition, freed from its shackles, may itself be part of an Enlightenment heritage and thus, ironically, another manifestation of "tradition"[9] at work.

One source of the dichotomy between experience and tradition, firsthand religion versus mere understanding and/or "borrowed" religion is the American Evangelical Protestant heritage. This would thoroughly surprise the psychological writers, most of whom assume that Western religion has always focused on belief and ignored experience (in contrast, they often claim, to religion in the East). But nevertheless, it is in American popular piety, especially forms emphasizing a personal conversion experience, that James' division between first- and secondhand religion has its chief source.[10] This is not to say that the distinction between "direct experience" and "knowledge about" played no role in prior religion. Sentiments such as

> I had heard of thee by the hearing of the ear
> But now my eye sees thee;
> Therefore I despise myself
> And repent in dust and ashes (Job 42:5–6)

indicate the contrary. What made Evangelical and especially revival oriented piety so distinctive was its polemical stance against the kind of Christian commitment which relied on mere "hearing of the ear," and its insistence that direct personal experience of Jesus' saving power was an absolute prerequisite for truly being a Christian. This direct personal experience was a "conversion"; a conversion rather than knowledge of and assent to Christian doctrines was what counted. Conversions were a necessity for all, and potentially accessible to all. No Gestalt therapist or counterculture spokesperson could have been more the enemy of "head knowledge" than the revivalists of the last century, and Evangelical Christians today have often continued this emphasis.

Within the religious world of Evangelical Protestantism, a conversion experience could be located in time and space; thus the image of a commemorative plaque would be thoroughly appropriate. Dramatic and intense, the conversion involved an about-face in one's relationship with God. Usually preceded by a period of inner torment, self-loathing, and guilt over one's sinfulness, the moment of conversion meant liberation.

> Although up to that moment my soul had been filled with indescribable gloom, I felt the glorious brightness of the noonday sun shine into my heart. I felt I was a free man. Oh, the precious feeling of safety, of freedom, of resting on Jesus! I felt that Christ with all

his brightness and power had come into my life; that indeed, old things had passed away and all things had become new.[11]

This experience becomes the foundation for a new stage in the individual's existence; one is "born again" into a life of freedom in Christ. What is intriguing is the closeness of the above account (which is typical of many thousands of conversion reports) to the testimonies of contemporary persons who consider themselves utterly alienated from traditional religion. For instance, a woman speaks of

> an almost mystical experience of renewal, where body and soul seem to be perfectly integrated, existence is given meaning and immortality is somehow affirmed.[12]

Although the experience in the second case is sexual orgasm, and the author hostile or indifferent to conventional religion, the language and the set of ideas about the ultimacy of inner experience echo the nineteenth century Protestant convert's. One is strongly tempted to think of a basic psychological state of intense renewal, which is triggered by various circumstances and interpreted in divergent ways.

One difference on which the inner experience advocates would insist is that the Christian convert was never entirely liberated from a specific religious tradition. Jesus remained the corner-stone of faith; the phrase "old things had passed away and all things had become new" certainly shows the experiencer's familiarity with a tradition and its scriptures. Moreover, the whole rationale for conversion depended on a set of beliefs about man's innate sinfulness, and the necessity of redemption by a savior. In other words, the contemporary psychological advocate of inner experience would view even the most fervent Christian convert as too dependent on tradition, on socially derived beliefs and expectations. In contrast, the claims for liberating transcendent sexuality come from "the experience itself" and not from any traditional and inherited teachings about the nature of reality. This, at least, would be the reply of most inner experience advocates to our parallel between their own spirituality and that of popular Protestant piety.

Since the issue of what constitutes the experience itself will arise often in the next chapters, we alert the reader to the fact that this is a matter for much debate. Some of the more perceptive writers will argue that ideas and attitudes brought to the experience itself play a major role in shaping its content. Others will insist that direct experience gives meaning prior to all interpretations and cultural expectations, that anyone having the experience will apprehend certain values or truths which are intrinsic to it. At this point, however, we wish only to suggest an ancestry for today's claims about direct experience, an ancestry unknown to most psychological writers.

Such antecedents disprove one of the most popular claims of inner experience writers: that Americans have always been hostile to inwardness, and that American life and religion have been one-sidedly extroverted. American religion has not been contemplative, but it has often risked one-sided devotion to eliciting conversion experiences. Certainly, American popular Protestantism never put the kind of emphasis on mere doctrine or empty ritual claimed by psychological critics. In fact, accusations against a secondhand religiousness of mere externals were and are the stock in trade of the Evangelical advocate. We are not, however, trying to explain away psychological ideas about religion and experience by showing them to be dependent on Christianity, a kind of reduction which would distort the intentions of psychological writers to provide an alternative to traditional faiths.

If Protestant revivalism is a source for beliefs about the primacy of inner experience, are there others? Consider the Western romantic love ideal, in which deep inner emotions justify the entire existence of the lover. Falling in love is an inner experience for which another person serves as the trigger, and it is an experience which everyone in our society is expected to have for him/herself. Like conversion, it was publicized in nineteenth century popular culture, and like conversion is out of style with today's psychological writers. One might speculate that interest in other inner experiences might be prompted by increasing disillusionment with romantic love, or at least with romantic love as an adequate basis for a lifelong commitment to another person.

We shall meet with various statements, restatements and refinements of the trust in direct experience throughout the next six chapters. We will also explore the diversity of psychological systems which have been generated to make sense of particular experiences. We will also occasionally look to the past, to see if consistency exists between past and present perceptions of the meanings of the experience itself. Throughout, we will insist on the religious and moral dimensions of contemporary claims on behalf of inner experiences, rather than the "scientific" value of current perspectives.

Dreams and
Ordinary Life

The following passage expresses a view of dreams widely held in contemporary Western culture:

> The thought keeps suggesting itself (the insane thought par excellence) that, perhaps, the bright reality of everyday life is but an illusion, to be swallowed up at any moment by the howling nightmares of the other, the night side of reality.[1]

DREAMING TODAY

This view is opposed by inner experience advocates, who offer visions and evaluations of the experience and meaning of dreams. In this chapter, we will attend to their pleas on behalf of a more positive and constructive understanding of these howling nightmares. To many people in our culture, dreams signify a terrifying chaotic otherness which lurks forever at the borders of the rational world of daytime, the world in which we feel at home. It is this view that current advocates for dreaming universally oppose, on the grounds that it is paranoid, repressive, and fundamentally untrue to the real nature of dreams. Yet many of them will accept a symbolic division between "day-world" (light, reason, normalcy) and the "night-world" (the domain of other forces). Where they would violently disagree with the common view is in the evaluation of these two worlds. Another set of writers would try to breach the gap, on the grounds that ultimately, the world of dreaming and the world of waking are one. A third aspect of the challenge to the howling nightmares view of dreams is to subtly convey a sense of everyday life (the day-world) as itself frightening and chaotic.

Current writings on dreams include two separate groups of materials: laboratory studies, mostly on the physiology of dreaming, and works which address the psychological question, What do dreams mean? Although the laboratory research has made the study of dreaming scientifically respectable, it does not generally address itself to questions about the meaning of dreaming as an experience, let alone provide answers to inquiries about what particular dreams mean. Laboratory studies of dreaming have shown that everyone dreams four to five times a night, and that dreaming is not in any sense "caused" by factors external to the organism. Although people vary greatly in the degree to which they recall dreams, no consistently discovered personality factors seem to separate recallers from nonrecallers. Most dreams occurring under sleep lab conditions are far from howling nightmares; they are often extraordinarily prosaic. The more pictorial kind of dreams are generally linked to REM (rapid eye movement) sleep but some thinking occurs even under non-REM conditions.

From the viewpoint of those interested in the meaningfulness of dreams (especially the popular writers) the above information means that dreaming is a normal and healthy occurrence. According to popular writers, if we can recall some dreams, and if dreams are important, then we ought to strive to recall them, and assume that if we fail to do so, we are repressing or we lack confidence in our dreams. Here the objectively ascertained prevalence of an experience becomes transmuted into a distinctly moral claim that the experience is "normal" or at least non-threatening. Actually, beyond these few basic facts, remarkably little use is made of laboratory findings by those who write for general audiences on the mysterious power of dreams.

Since we are concerned with the experience of dreaming—how it is understood as a human situation, its moral and religious dimensions—we will overlook the criterion of scientific validity altogether. It may well be that "What do dreams mean?" is simply not a legitimate scientific question. "How to get the most from your dreams" is one of the goals of most writers whose works we will discuss; a coherent psychological theory of dreaming is not presented. While even the most how-to-do-it writer depends on some theory about dreams, the theory is usually rudimentary and unconnected with even the trappings of science.

Another dimension to the extreme practicality of the psychological approach to dreaming is the overall lack of interest in the metaphysics or epistemology of dreams. Dreams are meaningful and helpful; whether they are ultimately real or more real than waking life is not considered a problem. "The insane thought par excellence" does not trouble most contemporary advocates of dreaming. Although there is a great deal of interest in the relation between day-world and night-world, it does not focus on the classic philosophical issue of illusion versus reality. Instead, it takes a moral form: the problem of dreaming and waking becomes a problem of self-deception versus self-awareness. If dreams speak the truth and reveal our innermost feelings, should we trust them to guide us? Or should we continue to block out their messages and rely only on our rational waking thoughts? Dreams can have real

effects, they are important, they have spiritual significance—but all these claims can be made while bypassing
the metaphysical status of dreams. Is it necessary to be
more philosophically oriented than was Havelock Ellis
when he remarked, "Dreams are true while they last. Can
we at the best say more of life?"[2]

In contrast, the moral and psychological relation between dream worlds and the world of waking life does
preoccupy inner experience advocates. They claim that if
one ignores or dismisses the direct experience of dreams,
then one arrives at the view quoted at the beginning of the
chapter. Dreams will take on a fearful power, and be seen
as agents of chaos best hidden from consciousness. This
view is perceived as the dominant one of our "dream-
thieving society"; at a personal level its results are a disas-
trous constricting of our own human possibilities. In contrast, as book titles such as *Dreams Are Your Truest
Friends*[3] and *Dreams: Your Magic Mirror*[4] indicate, advocates of dreaming see attentiveness to dreams as reward-
ing, enriching, and transformative. Instead of howling
nightmares, the dreamer will experience something powerful yet beneficent. Ultimately, dreaming, when taken
seriously, will lead to improvements in one's day-world
existence. And for many psychological writers, that ordinary waking reality is experienced as anything but bright
and reassuring.

There are thus two principle paths for rehabilitating
dreaming as a human experience. The first accepts a dichotomy between day and night worlds, but reevaluates it.
This approach depends on the dream remaining in some
sense alien to the self. Psychologically, such a view sees
dreams as having a compensatory relation to waking consciousness. The other view stresses the unity of dreaming
and waking selves and attempts to assimilate dreaming
into the bright world of clear and certain purposes and
rational control. This view relies on a perceived continuity
between dreams and waking. Somewhat disconcerting is

the lack of awareness shown by those inner experience advocates who claim the benefits of both views, without recognizing the differences in their psychological and moral implications. This lack of awareness, however, may be evidence of a genuine ambivalence over the moral worth of contemporary existence.

DREAMS AS MINIREVELATIONS

In the context of religion, the term "revelation" is used to signify an encounter with a numinous Other, or with some force or principle experienced as ultimate. Revelation assumes that this encounter is normative and binding on all. Current rehabilitators of dreams, however, do not make this kind of religious claim. But throughout the psychological literature, dreams are perceived as minirevelations; messages or gifts from a "Whence," they are seen as binding and more or less authoritative for the dreamer alone. This perspective allows for a variety of specific formulations, from "God speaks to us through dreams" to "Dreams put us in touch with the True Self." These formulations promote an attitude of trustful receptivity, whatever the Whence from which dreams originate. Dreams are actively demanding of our attention, and their presence is ultimately for our own well-being. The proper attitude to take is one of respect and attentive listening.

To see dreams as helpful messages from a Whence is neither recent nor limited to psychologists. Current dream literature relies on two sources for this view: the first can be labeled "folk tradition," while the second is an Americanized and somewhat tamed version of Jungian psychology. These two blend together readily, especially since many writers are not too concerned about the exact nature of the Whence which sends dreams. Folk tradition goes back many hundreds of years and has its roots in the ancient world. Through the ages, it has treated dreams as coded messages, warnings, or predictions sent by gods or by God to help the dreamer. These messages might concern external conditions (accidents) or internal predicaments (a psychological crisis not being faced honestly by the dreamer). Although allowances were made for specific life circumstances, on the whole the coding was impersonal and universal, hence, "dictionaries" of dream symbols, which even find their way into several contemporary psychologically oriented self-help books on dreams. In fact, much of the self-help literature might well be described as a direct continuation of this ancient folk tradition, with a veneer of psychology added.

When the topic is prophetic or telepathic dreams, or dreams of the dead, folk tradition continues without modification in contemporary literature. For some of today's dream advocates, all dreams of this nature illustrate the mysterious power and truthfulness of the dream; there is little demand for belief in dead spirits or telepathy. The helpfulness of the dream is what counts. For instance, one writer tells the following dream: a daughter sees her dead mother drowning in a pool. The mother says, "Daughter, these are the tears you have shed for me. Let me go, for I am drowning in them."[5] The clear message to stop mourning does not depend on the dreamer or reader choosing whether the dream comes from the daughter's unconscious or the dead mother's spirit. What matters is that the dream itself is a gift, a sign of a presence outside our conscious control.

Contemporary advocates of dreaming as inner experience who wish to employ a psychological theory generally rely (more or less directly) on that of Carl Jung. Although a hard-core Jungian might repudiate many of the restatements of Jung's dream theories which are made by inner experience advocates, it is Jung's writings that provide a clear psychological rationale for taking dreams seriously and for trusting them. Dreams, in Jung's eyes, are the voice of the unconscious, the other and alien part of the self. The unconscious reveals, manifesting itself even in a world dominated by rationality and bent on repressing everything mythic, intuitive, archaic, and sacred. As a critic of Western rationalism, Jung gave dreams the enormous role of returning the lost secular ego to its hidden spiritual roots.[6]

What makes Jung's view so close to the folk tradition and so useful as a defense of dreams is that for Jung the unconscious is ultimately trustworthy and wise. In Freudian thought, the dream, as we remember it, is the end product of a long and tortuous process of "dream-work," involving censorship, disguise, and displacement. This process makes it difficult for us to become aware of the dream-thoughts, which are very different from the remembered manifest dream content. For Freud, the unconscious is tricky and deceptive; for Jung, it wants to communicate, although its language of images is alien to our rational minds. It is this difference which seems to make Jung's thought so very appealing to popular advocates of dreaming, whatever the stated reason they offer for rejecting Freud. For Jung and contemporary advocates, repression is something we (our rational egos) choose to do with a dream. For Freud, repression is at work within the dream itself.

Jung's position was that the conscious (waking) mind and the unconscious (dreaming) mind complement each other. The unconscious acts as a corrective to consciousness, balancing the ego's views with its own perceptions of the dreamer's situation. If one accepts this formulation of the relation of day and night realities, it is not hard to see how dreams could become "your truest friends." The experience of dreaming is a gateway to a whole new side of yourself. Hitherto unknown, and still alien, this hidden you can be discovered and appreciated via the dream. And here the complementarity thesis opens the door for unlimited (and magical) hopes as to the nature of this other self. It might be filled with all sorts of creative potentials unknown to our ordinary day selves.

Dreams certainly do reveal us in our true colors, but
these colors can be light as well as dark, gay as well
as drab, beautiful as well as ugly. While they undoubtedly do sometimes ask us to face up to problems
we are trying to bury, it is much more important to
emphasize the positive function of the dream, which
is to show us why we get into difficulties in waking
life.[7]

The lost self then could be more spiritual, closer to one's
ideal, than the waking self.

But is this lost self truly us? Or is it alien, "Other"—as
Jung's theory of the collective unconscious suggests? The
True Self of popular advocates of dreaming is never so
clearly not-me. It is closer to a wise and friendly guide.
Ann Faraday, the best of the popular writers, can write:
"How much better to take advice from the other half of
yourself than from another person,"[8] a definite domestica-
tion of Jungian Otherness. Other writers feel free to talk
about "the need to improve or conquer various aspects of
Self"[9] or to describe a dream as "a letter to ourselves from
our Self."[10] Here, all that remains of Jung's original ideal
of a superior, universal alien power is the capital S for
Self. In all fairness, Jung's theory was based on his own
dreams and those of his patients, all of whom were under-
going profound dislocations of their ordinary sense of
themselves, and so perhaps overestimated the alien nature of the dreaming self.

Can we be more specific about this True Self? Is it the
"Whence" of dreams, which few advocates of dreaming
care to discourse on? Other "Whence" terms include God,
"the superconscious," and a gentle divinity called "Dream
Power" by the imaginative Ann Faraday. These powers
are evoked and praised; an attitude of trustful receptivity
toward them is urged. Plenty of room is left for traditional
religious beliefs, so that a conservative Christian can advocate "a restoration of faith in dreams as a vehicle of the

message of God in order to receive guidance from Him"[11] without sounding very different from any of the more psychologically oriented authors. Clearly, terms like "True Self" are closer to God than to empirical constructs in a systematic personality theory. They are symbols of transcendence, not psychological categories such as defense mechanism or cognitive dissonance. Put simply, it does not matter if the "Whence" of dreams is God, the unconscious, or the True Self; all that is being claimed by inner experience advocates is that the dream puts us in touch with the really Real.

Trustful receptivity toward inner experience is the overarching theme of contemporary psychological advocates. Trustful receptivity in regard to dreams shows itself in any number of ways. Foremost is the faith that the dream force itself provides answers, solutions to problems, and comfort. The following three statements of this faith should speak for themselves:

Thank you, dream power, for the dream of the island (or whatever) you sent last night. I feel it's an important dream, but despite all my efforts, I'm still unable to get the message. Please send me another dream tonight putting the same message in a way I can understand.[12]

An open relaxed state of being. . . . It can be likened to fishing. The conscious mind is rod and line. The dream is the bait, the question the hook. These are lowered into the waters of the unconscious by becoming quiet and passive, letting the question and dream sink into lower levels of consciousness by stilling the upper levels. Then, like the fisherman, one has to be patient. One waits for the line to pull. It is no use thinking.[13]

As we have learned to give our conscious selves over to God, and trust our thought, so we can also commit our unconscious to Him for His protection of His message through dreams.[14]

Here is that symbolic withinness which inner experience writers cherish and hope to strengthen. It is both fragile and awe-inspiring, hidden from sight yet always active. In a world of at best ambiguous moral dilemmas, the "Whence" of dreams is always trustworthy.

HOW TO GET THE MOST FROM DREAMS

If the only attitude toward dreaming among contemporary advocates were that of trustful receptivity, we would be safer in calling contemporary dream psychologies continuations of the folk tradition. However, the same authors who extol dreams as messages from the True Self are not really happy with patience and passivity. Once one takes dreams seriously, one is compelled to do something with or to them, to work with them in some way. In many cases, this will lead to a manipulative approach toward dreaming and the self. At one extreme, some authors are fascinated by the possibility of tinkering with the dream from within. In the following passage, the emphasis is on control over one's own inner experience, and the imagery is suitably technological.

> Our thoughts, daydreams, and dreams have remained a mystery to us and have been erroneously viewed as having a life of their own, independent of us and beyond our control. Estranged from ourselves, few of us have come to realize that *we* largely select and feed the "programs" to be daily processed by our remarkable brain-computers ... programs which can work for us or against us.[15]

Yet this approach, no less than the first, takes dreams seriously. Moreover, many popular writers will claim the benefits of both trustful receptivity and a tinkering attitude without sensing any incongruity. If the issue is perceived as a choice between two psychological theories, a

Jungian view and a theory which insists on continuity between the waking and dreaming self, the difficulty of holding both views is obvious. Either dreams represent something mysterious and other, or they are products of the same old daytime me and cannot function as a storehouse of wisdom. The latter view, a "continuity hypothesis" of the relation between dreams and waking behavior, is held in stark form by Hall and Nordby, who have done massive statistical studies of dreaming. In their findings:

> Skiers dream of skiing, surfers dream of surfing and mountain climbers dream of climbing mountains. Teachers dream of classroom situations, bankers dream of banking activities and nurses dream about their patients. Alcoholics dream of drinking, child molesters dream of molesting children, and arsonists dream of setting fires. . . .
>
> The dream world is neither discontinuous nor inverse in its relationship to the conscious world. We remain the same person, the same personality with the same characteristics and the same basic beliefs and convictions, whether awake or asleep.[16]

Such a position will disappoint those who hope to gain access to a hidden self through dreams, but it does have an implication which some popular writers find important. If there is a basic continuity between dreams and waking, then changing dream behavior may "carry over" into changes in waking life.[17] For instance, programming oneself to be successful in a dream may lead to self-confidence in waking life. Here dreams are very significant as a private testing ground for self-transformation. Very often, some trace of the first view is retained as an elusive expectation. For instance, the same authors who were sure that we ourselves program our dreams will hold that with proper attentiveness to dreaming, "Debilitating personality thorns can be detected and uprooted while long-neglected creative and intuitive potentials are encouraged to blossom."[18] Notice how technological metaphors give way to pleasing natural ones; "creative potentials" have life and growth of their own, even if it is ultimately the rational ego which distinguishes them from "debilitating personality thorns."

But even modern writers who are more Jungian in that they respect the otherness of the dream, are activist and work-oriented in their "getting the most from dreams" approach. To begin with, dreamers must learn to recall and record their dreams, and most popular writers include careful step-by-step directions for doing this. Then comes interpretation, which is also systematic and rationalized, whatever the exact school of interpretation. Sometimes interpretation in the classic sense is less important than "dream games," a playful and more light-hearted approach—but even here the goal is to gain awareness and control over one's inner experiences. Whatever the technique(s) recommended, the idea is to *do* something with dreams, to create a climate in which dreams are gradually integrated into the rational, orderly world of waking. Only then can one obtain true benefits from dreaming.

> From these dreams you can gain understanding of your own inner nature. To know yourself better is to confront, understand and gradually accept your innermost feelings. You thereby can begin to liberate yourself from the tyranny of unconscious "shoulds" and "don'ts" with their endless and unnecessary torments of punishments and worries.[19]

For those who find this how-to, activist, and occasionally manipulative posture an affront to the unconscious and its wisdom, we will offer several possible defenses. First, many laboratory studies of dreaming have shown that the majority of dreams are neither exciting, dreamlike, nor particularly worth remembering. We forget them because they are unmemorable and not necessarily because of repression. A perceptive and philosophically oriented author admits that our attitudes toward dreams may be the key to what goes on within the dreaming state; if dreams are considered worthless, they will be so, whereas "by investing dreams with a wealth of potential meaning and acting accordingly, they can become equal in usefulness and inspiration to the deepest forms of creative thought."[20] Thus, some deliberate reprogramming of our cultural attitudes may be required before dreams become significant. Jung's psychological theory would create revised expectations about dreams, which in turn would make the dreams themselves more exciting. If some set of beliefs creating high expectations for dreams is needed in order for dreams to become significant, then the experience itself will not be sufficient to generate theories and expectations.

Another argument used by advocates of how-to-do-it approaches to dreaming is to claim that most persons today do feel victimized and unable to control their own lives. To instill an attitude of self-confidence and self-direction is to help those people function more effectively. An excellent route to this goal is to train people to take control of their dreams, precisely because dreaming has so long been seen as the activity of the mysterious other, the out-of-our-control situation par excellence. If we can see our dreams as ours, as manageable by us, then this will be a major victory over victimhood. Instead of being at the mercy of howling nightmares, we will be able to overcome them.

The creative dreamer's greatest advantage over the ordinary dreamer is his continuous opportunity to unify his personality. The fearlessness of dream images . . . produces a mood of capability that carries over into waking life, providing a foundation for confident, capable action.[21]

This answer is such a pervasive one in all self-help literature that we shall find variants of it throughout the next chapters. The two assumptions are (1) awareness is the key to control over behavior and (2) change is possible and relatively easy. The second assumption is necessary, for most inner experience writers are (to put it mildly) skeptical of psychotherapists and other so-called experts, who are perceived as impediments to self-sufficiency. ("It is essential, then, that we learn to be our own dream authorities.")[22] The assumption is that any sincere and hardworking individual can reshape his personality—get rid of those thorns—and that only a few problems are too deep-seated to be overcome without outside help. Learning to take one's dreams seriously will benefit everyone. When we know how to get our dreams to work for us we will have the awareness necessary to become more fully functioning human beings.

The very essence of this ethic appears with the possibility of controlling the dream from within, while it is in the act of being dreamed. This is called "lucid dreaming" in current literature; for Westerners it represents a brand-new idea, an extension of manipulation to an experience previously considered beyond our will to control. According to enthusiastic proponents of lucid dreaming, the active controlling of dreams was standard practice among a tribe in Malaysia, the Senoi. There, children were carefully trained to conquer the monsters encountered in dreams and otherwise bend the dream events to their own interests. Reliable information on the Senoi is scarce,[23] but as a model for what it would mean to take dreams seriously, they have become heroes of contemporary dream writings. The Senoi apparently accepted dreams as minirevelations and sought to control them, thereby becoming heroes for popular writers of a Jungian persuasion as well. Whatever the actual truth about the Senoi, lucid dreaming in an American context is a means toward vanquishing those howling night-

mares on their home turf. "Achieving positive outcomes"
for all dream situations is what one writer means by
"creative dreaming."[24]

There are times when lucid dreaming can be something
more than positive thinking imported into one's dreams. It
makes the dream a miniworld in which all things are
possible. As a testimony to this, here is a lucid dream of the
present writer. I had been wondering about the deceptive-
ness of childhood memories; North Salem is the little vil-
lage where I spent summers as a child:

> A dream of flying—just by flapping my arms. It was
> beautiful. We were back in North Salem. I was inside
> a basement and felt leaden and dizzy. Then I told
> myself, "This is a dream. You ought to be able to fly."
> I started concentrating and left the ground, headed
> for the ceiling. I found a broken window, removed the
> screen and climbed out. And then soared above the
> huge locust trees and across the road. The evening
> sky was clear and warm, but there were soft electric
> lights on some of the trees, and a chandelier in the
> sky.

In this dream, lucidity is concretized by the light bulbs and
chandelier. The dream itself affirms the transcendence of
memory over time and space, and also the freedom to rise
above one set of memories (the basement) and reclaim
another (tall trees and clear sky). There may be a limit to
the amount of manipulation which can be imposed on a
dream, or there may be good reasons for refraining from
tinkering with the dream content. But I would affirm the
unique sense of freedom and mystery acquired during
lucid dreaming, in which the dreamer can briefly become
a god in creating a private world. Within my dream I can
fly, ride a bicycle expertly, and even reverse sequences of
behavior. This is not a statement about hidden potentials
but about the nature of dreaming itself.

DREAMING AND LIBERATION

We have focused in this chapter less on the dream as experience than on the symbolic dichotomy between the waking world and the dream world. It seems that this dichotomy lies behind, and is challenged by many of the psychological pleas on behalf of dreams. So long as the waking world is experienced as bright and orderly, dreams are forced to represent howling chaotic otherness. On the other hand, if it is our waking world which makes us feel victimized and out of control, then dreams might be a means for us to reestablish order on our own terms, to exert control successfully. The dream itself may not be one thing or the other. There are even cases of insomniacs who could not tell if they had been dreaming or just thinking (they claimed to be awake and thinking while the EEG showed them to be sound asleep). Without question, all dreams are not dreamlike in the sense of naturally bizarre and chaotic. Nor are all waking thoughts rational. At the psychological level then, it may be that dreams are flexible, adapting to our expectations or hopes for them. If these hopes are contradictory or are flatly unrealistic, we can and will be disappointed (it is not truly a hidden potential to fly by flapping one's arms). Dreams may, however, be more mirror-like than fixed in function or contents.

But if dreams depend on context and expectations, it is up to us not merely to get the most from dreams but to give them our best. And if we are genuinely threatened and confused in our waking, social experience, will we be more likely to discover security, strength and peace in our dreams? It is no good citing the famous cases of creative discovery in dreams to answer this question. Only a skilled chemist could solve a chemical problem by dreaming of it; only a talented poet could dream an original poetic masterpiece. A child molester and an arsonist do not avoid or overcome their antisocial activities, but repeat them in dreams. Perhaps the belief in a helpful, friendly True Self is something of a self-fulfilling prophecy, and perhaps it is evidence for a pervasive feeling of inadequacy and dependence on magical solutions which will not be overcome by pinning one's hopes on dreams.

Without a doubt, dream experience can enhance waking life. What many inner experience advocates seem to be asking is that it rescue us from waking life—and ultimately from our ordinary, boring, mundane selves. This is setting up an opposition between the realm of the authentic, the really Real, and all else, an opposition which pervades so much of the inner experience literature. Even the most technologically oriented popular writers hope that at the heart of dream experience one will be able to reach a level of reality which "has been variously referred to as Being, God, All That Is, and the Universal Mind."[25] But in order to get there one must first admit to the basically unsatisfactory and inhospitable nature of ordinary life.

This does not imply an ethic of withdrawal from the world, or of revolutionary alienation from its social arrangements. After all, getting your dreams to work for you can mean achieving such obviously worldly goals as a better marriage or a promotion. But it is not enough to promise merely these, or so it seems. Dreams must do more than help adapt the individual to social reality; they must liberate at a spiritual level. Terms like "lucidity" and "awareness" signal this liberation; beliefs about the True Self and invocations of Dream Power do the same. In fact, the promise of liberation becomes ridiculous only when it is tied too closely to concrete benefits, as in the following claim:

The resources within each individual are unlimited. . . . The most satisfactory surprise is to know that we ourselves can "deliver the goods" and that there are lots more where they came from. To ride high, to enjoy, not to have to pay a price, and not to have to be a victim is the only way to live![26]

As a vision of some genuine Other condition this might have some validity, but as an expectation and an ethic for this world, it is both ludicrous and egocentric.

Dreams themselves do not provide automatic liberation. There is no more somber way to illustrate this than to draw on the collection of dreams made by Charlotte Beradt, dreams of persons living under the first years of Nazi rule. *The Third Reich of Dreams* (Chicago: Quadrangle Books), is an agonizing corroboration of Hall and Nordby's "continuity hypothesis." In a world where ordinary reality was being systematically destroyed, dreams like this one were common:

> It was about nine o'clock in the evening. My consultations were over, and I was just stretching out on a couch to relax with a book on Matthias Grunewald, when suddenly the walls of my room and then my apartment disappeared. I looked around and discovered to my horror that as far as the eye could see no apartment had walls anymore. Then I heard a loudspeaker boom, "According to the decree on the 17th of this month on the Abolition of Walls."[27]

Passivity and victimization were the rule in dreams, as in waking life. The members of underground groups, by contrast, dreamed of fleeing and outwitting the police. Without daytime courage and personal resources, dreams provided no relief or salvation or hidden potentials which could be carried over into waking behavior. Although Beradt's collection is impressionistic, it offers sobering counterevidence to the inner experience writers' enthusiastic hopes for dreams.

To inner experience advocates, dreams are for modern

persons only a starting point in the reclaiming of the world within. Other experiences are viewed as even further from normal ordinary reality, perhaps even insane in the most literal sense. The "howling nightmares" view is less often expressed than the more prosaic, "Don't worry —it was only a dream!" It may be the task of the inner experience authors who focus on dreams to question this attitude, by showing us how dreams are neither trivial, useless, nor childish. Other experiences we shall examine are not dismissed as irrelevant but are actively avoided or condemned. When this is the case, the easy union of folk tradition and contemporary rediscovery does not exist. And we shall find that what Western religion specifically condemned, inner experience advocates must sometimes glorify.

Daydreaming and the Protestant Ethic

In this chapter, we will turn to an experience which requires a far more extensive rehabilitation than dreaming. When advocates of dreams wished to bolster their views, they appealed to old and widespread folk tradition for support. In contrast, those who wish to rehabilitate daydreaming or waking fantasy for contemporary people have no such resource from the past. The newer literature on fantasy must deal with the legacy of mistrust and negative judgments which arises in almost everyone's mind when the subject of daydreaming is mentioned. However dreamlike many waking fantasies may be, they have about them a dubious, shameful air which night dreams do not share. The central reason for this seems to be that whereas night dreams are assumed to be outside our conscious control, our daytime waking thoughts are our own direct responsibility. For this reason, people are far more cautious about revealing daydreams than in telling their dreams of the night. At worst, dreams at night are something one cannot help experiencing; at best they are the voice of the lost True Self, as we have seen. Because we presumably can prevent ourselves from daydreaming, it is also harder to make a case for the daydream as a path to some alien inner me.

In the following discussion, we will use "daydream" and "waking fantasy" interchangeably and will spend some time discussing just what experiences are covered by these terms. Oddly, in order to rehabilitate the experience, some authors—particularly therapists—have drawn a sharp line between mere daydreaming and "waking dreams," "active imagination," or "directed daydreaming." The latter terms all describe a presumably healthy and soul-opening form of activity, whereas daydreaming is dismissed as a "degradation" of the imagination.[1] Among Jungian writers, it is just the control factor which makes this dichotomy possible; the more waking fantasy is spontaneous and "dreamlike," the more it too can be a vehicle for the unconscious. Ordinary daydreaming is presumed to be under the ego's control, and therefore worthless as a clue to deeper levels of the self. However, the present writer's belief is that such a dichotomy illustrates a moralistic and somewhat arrogant attitude toward mental life, which differs little from that taken by the mainstream culture.

It is a strong part of our cultural heritage to distrust and condemn daydreaming. One of the valid reasons for this is that a technologically complex world demands a high level of attentiveness from its citizens, a constant monitoring of the external environment. The drifting and relaxed mental state associated with fantasy is permissible when one is shelling peas, but it may be deadly on an assembly line or when driving a car. If daydreaming and waking dreams are advocated, it will be assumed that they will be appropriate only under certain special circumstances—such as waiting for a bus or during psychotherapy. These are some of the modern situations which do not call for full attentiveness to the external world.

But few persons in the West have condemned fantasy

because it might lead to traffic accidents. In order to discover the chief source of our suspicion of daydreaming, we must look back further, to the tradition of Calvinism and the Protestant ethic. Although the Protestant ethic was described by Max Weber in its relation to economic activity, it is on one level a mental attitude toward all activity, i.e., an attitude toward the self as well as the marketplace. Briefly, it demands a constant vigilance and scrutiny of both one's inner life and one's behavior. It suggests that, left unchecked, the mind would follow its own natural inclinations, forsake God and wallow in depravity. Unbridled, unruly thoughts must be curbed; an idle mind is a gateway for idolatry and blasphemy to pass through. In Calvin's words:

> Surely, just as waters boil up from a vast, full spring, so does an immense crowd of gods flow forth from the human mind, while each one, in wandering about with too much license, wrongly invents this or that about God Himself.[2]

This attitude toward the mind's spontaneous activity did not originate with Calvinism; it had been a staple of Western monasticism and Eastern ascetic spirituality. Where Calvin innovated was by adapting it to the daily life of all, making even the average person take on some of the mental orientation of the monk.

The means to do this was to discourage "idleness" of all kinds. Both mental play and physical play fell under strong strictures. Group play gradually became assimilated into the category of evil, ungodly activity (not for Calvin but for later Puritans), while mental play became "useless fancies." Weber's thesis in *The Protestant Ethic and the Spirit of Capitalism* is that there is a connection between this ethical and mental orientation and the rise of capitalism.[3] We may say that mental fantasy became not merely sinful, but unprofitable (for one's living as well as one's salvation). Daydreaming, the epitome of mental idleness, became linked to sensuality, temptation, and other moral dangers. Parents and school teachers were urged to guard their children from it. Women, considered weaker in spirit than men, were also thought to be more vulnerable to its enticements, and so were forbidden to read novels (which encouraged dreaminess and idleness). Psychologists have followed this tradition by labelling daydreams as escapist and by warning of the moral and psychic damage which addiction to this vice will produce.

Only recently have a few workers begun trying to make a case for fantasy. Many more are enthusiastic about the therapeutic benefits of special forms of fantasy (imagery therapies are popular today) while still holding ordinary daydreaming as suspect as the most rigorous Calvinist. Very often, the issue is seen as one of rehabilitating the world of the inner eye for a culture which is overly extroverted. The Puritan ethic, however, was not one of simple extroversion, but of scrupulous concern for inner life, coupled with a suspicion of its spontaneity. In taking on the task of rehabilitating fantasy, inner experience advocates are challenging a major strand of Western moral and religious tradition. Is their alternative adequate to meet genuine human needs? Should we disregard entirely the Calvinist suspicion of fantasy?

In order to assess the advocacy of waking fantasy, we need to know what kinds of experiences are at stake, rather than remain content with generalized notions of daydreaming and its supposedly pernicious influence. We will look at some scholarly research, then at an outspoken popular advocate of daydreaming. Only then can we raise the question of so-called higher forms of waking fantasy and their relationship to religion and the life of the spirit. As with dreams, we will consider the claim that fantasy liberates—and as with dreams we will have to ask, From what and for what?

THE NATURE OF WAKING FANTASY

Investigating spontaneous fantasy in ordinary individuals proved an elusive task for psychologists. Although part of depth therapy relied upon free association, this was never equated with fantasy. In the 1930s, a psychological test which asked subjects to make up stories about a standardized set of pictures (the Thematic Apperception Test) was created as a test of fantasy, but this is clearly a different human situation from that of the solitary daydreamer. And due to the vague link between dreams, play, and daydreaming, it was assumed that all three represented what Freudians call "primary process thinking." That meant that these activities were under the sway of an illogical, regressive "pleasure principle" which was hostile to realistic thought. Fantasy was assumed to be wish-fulfilling, egocentric, pictorial rather than abstract, and often bizarre in its contents.[4] A large amount of psychological information on it came from patients in therapy, but it was assumed that everyone's daydreaming shared these qualities.

In order to discover whether this portrait of daydreaming was accurate, a new approach was necessary. Two researchers have made outstanding contributions to the study of daydreaming, both of them challenging the general psychological assumptions about its nature and functions. The more experimentally-oriented, Eric Klinger, trained subjects to think aloud in order to record sequences in their thought processes. Klinger defined fantasy as "all mentation whose ideational products are not evaluated by the subject in terms of their usefulness in advancing some immediate goal extrinsic to the mentation itself."[5] This means that fantasy is something all of us engage in throughout the day. It can alternate easily with task oriented thought, as subjects work on puzzles and then comment to themselves, "Holy buckets! I never understand these things!" Fantasy is defined as a kind of

mental behavior, which for Klinger is "respondent" rather
than "operant," "ballistic" rather than "guided." "It is
hurled forward at each juncture by the new processes
cued off by its preceding content, but its aim is blind and
unintentional."[6] Subjectively, this will correspond to the
"effortless" quality of fantasy, and its unconcern with direct impact on the environment.[7] Thus, lack of vigilance
is, in Klinger's view, an essential attribute of fantasy,
whereas bizarreness, pictorial quality, and wish fulfillment are not. Klinger's study is an example of how a creative redefinition of a phenomenon may help uncover the
laws that govern its functioning. At the same time, Klinger's study reveals how the more spectacular and bizarre
forms of fantasy have received a lion's share of attention,
excluding the more mundane and forgettable thought sequences which Klinger's definition also covers.

Another psychologist who has done a great deal to study
and rehabilitate daydreaming is Jerome Singer, beginning with a book titled *Daydreaming: An Introduction to
the Experimental Study of Inner Experience* (Random
House, 1966). Based primarily on surveys and research
studies, this book stresses the varieties of daydream experience, its noncorrelation with pathology, and its many
functions in everyday life. According to these surveys, everyone daydreams, but the content and style of daydreaming vary. Some daydreams are wish oriented, some create
anxiety, and some are mildly pleasant without much connection to deep-seated personality needs or motives. Eth-
nic group membership seems to affect the amount of reported daydreaming, with Italians, Blacks, and Jews more
frequent daydreamers than other groups (the Irish, however, report more "fantastical" fantasies).[8] Though the interpretation of this finding is debatable (is it a question of
distance from the Protestant ethic?) the neglect of this sort
of data by many popular writers might reveal their own
bias toward a white, North European norm, or their com-

plete indifference to ethnicity as an authentic element in human identity.

Another interesting finding reported by Singer is that daydreaming activity falls into several distinct patterns. There are persons whose daydreams take the form of objective, controlled thoughtfulness, closely resembling operant problem-solving thought and neither imageful nor bizarre. There are others who report the more conventional "pictures in my head" dramatic sequences. Other patterns include several more questionable forms, "self-recriminating" and "body-centered rumination." For some persons, to fantasize means to attend to repeated self-inflicted insults or to worry that a vague pain might actually be undiagnosed cancer. It is not clear how these forms of fantasy fulfill wishes or offer escape. Still another pattern is described by Singer as "kaleidoscopic," and "The person scoring high on this pattern characterizes himself as showing marked distractability, depression, self-debasement, easy boredom and fleeting, vague thoughts."[9] Such a person finds inner consciousness confusing and distracting, and will turn to outside stimulation whenever boredom threatens.

But the type of experience still centrally associated with daydreaming is a long, relatively complex visionary sequence, an interior movie which one (effortlessly) scripts and directs for one's own enjoyment. The contents can range from "future interpersonal behavior" of the most ordinary sort to epics of heroic achievement, Messianic identification, and family murder.[10] Singer's book included some adolescent daydreams of his own, as a sample of what an achievement-oriented and well-adjusted young person would concoct by way of self-entertainment.

The most famous literary example of this form of daydreaming comes not from psychological research but from a short story, "The Secret Life of Walter Mitty," by James Thurber.[11] This tale shows the daydreamer as a henpecked, befuddled but utterly endearing fellow whose secret life consists of imaginary adventures as a naval plane commander, a famous surgeon, a star witness at a murder trial. The sequences are triggered by accidental features of Mitty's drab real world environment; the plots and characters are borrowed from popular culture. But the charm of this story is that Thurber makes sympathetic a kind of behavior universally condemned by Puritan-influenced psychologists and overwhelmingly perceived as shameful by the culture at large. This is exactly the kind of inner experience which is ordinarily equated with daydreaming.

In defense of the daydreamer, one could argue that his or her behavior is not overtly destructive or anti-social. A skilled daydreamer will not be bored waiting for the bus, or performing a monotonous task. He or she will not become restless when removed from a radio or television. In fact, even Walter Mitty is self-sufficient and independent insofar as he can draw from his own resources for comfort and entertainment. A habitual daydreamer is much more at home with inner life, whereas:

> Many persons who have failed to indulge in fantasy play may misinterpret vivid daydreams or images as hallucinations and be made far more anxious by the sudden, seemingly autonomous occurrence of a fantasy image.[12]

Mitty, for instance, knew the difference between his public life as a resident of Waterbury, Connecticut, and his secret life, and was absolutely unlikely to confuse fantasy with reality.

Behind these and other arguments lies a challenge to the cultural ideal of the man of action, the person who is always relating to and shaping the external environment. Such a person fights when angry, acts first and thinks later, and is probably less sensuously aware than the dreamy poetic type on whom he looks down. Do we really want men of action in our complex world? (Is the James Bond or John Wayne ideal suitable for day-to-day living?) A person more reliant on inner experience may be able to try out in fantasy various solutions to problems, or resort to imaginary rather than physical violence in response to frustrations and insults. In other words, daydreaming can be seen as a step toward self-control, more and more necessary in an urban, anonymous environment. And as already mentioned, inner-experience advocates would argue that the world's most vivid appreciations of sensuality and the beauty of nature come not from men of action but from those creative artists who are familiar with daydreaming and at home with their own inner worlds.

On the other hand, it is possible to overdo this linkage between fantasy and creativity. Most advocates of fantasy assume that it is closely tied to creativity and define the latter too nebulously for psychological analysis. It is possible that fantasy can aid creative efforts, just as dreams can. As with dreams, however, one must be capable of creative thought or action when not daydreaming. However, Singer does see even the most ordinary kinds of daydreams as potentially of value for human relationships— perhaps as stepping stones for new and untried forms of behavior.

As an example of the latter possibility, "directed daydreaming" in psychotherapy deserves mention. Although therapists insist that what they are doing is entirely different from ordinary escapist fantasy, it appears to depend on the same inner processes. In one simple example, a woman patient, when asked to visualize her relationship with her husband, pictured a little bird in a clenched hand. The therapist suggested that she imagine the hand opening and the bird flying away free. But the patient reported that the bird would not venture far away; it was a "sugar bird" that fed on sugar provided by humans, having forgotten how to get food for itself.[13] The therapist, correcting the ballistic flow of fantasy, suggested that the patient see the bird gradually learning to find food for itself. This example does involve an intervention from outside, but since the woman recognized the meaning of the sugar bird image (her problems were due to over-dependence on her husband) it is possible that she might have been able to transform the fantasy sequence on her own. At any rate, this rehearsal in imagery of a new relationship with her husband led to an immediate improvement in their marriage. Although daydreaming itself may be effortless and aimless, the task-oriented self may find ingenious uses for spontaneous mentation, as well as ways to influence the latter.

Advocating Fantasy

Singer's and Klinger's writings are scientifically reputable, based on experimental evidence of various kinds, and modest in the claims made on behalf of daydreaming. But when a popular writer wants to publicize the joys of fantasy, the results are quite different. The writer in question is Nancy Friday, whose book *My Secret Garden: Women's Sexual Fantasies* (New York: Pocket Books) sold several million copies and produced a sequel and many imitators. Ms. Friday's main confrontation was not with old-fashioned sexual puritanism, but with those modern puritans who would separate "real sex" (healthy) from "sexual fantasies" (neurotic). With stunning simplicity, she argues:

> Who needs fantasies? What's the matter with good, old-fashioned sex?
> Nothing's the matter with good, old-fashioned sex. Nothing's the matter with asparagus either. But why not have the hollandaise, too?[14]

The pleasures of fantasy enhance and accompany those of the external world, rather than interfere with them.

> This book is designed to win you over, unequivocally, first to the idea of female sexual fantasy as an introduction to love play, and eventually to the validity of sexual fantasy at any time.[15]

Fantasy is valid because it enhances pleasure, and also prepares a woman for new sexual roles and activities which she had previously believed forbidden to "nice people."

This book exudes a pornographic atmosphere, not solely ascribable to the contents of the fantasies themselves. *My Secret Garden* makes public what had always been private and shameful. "Women can share in their sisters' secrets and not feel that they are alone," proclaims the cover, and one of the intentions of the author is to give women reassurance, so that each woman "will no longer have that vertiginous fright that she alone has these random, often unbidden thoughts and ideas."[16] The material in the book can serve as a "yardstick . . . a sexual rule of thumb equivalent to that which men have always provided for themselves";[17] it can also serve as a wealth of suggestions for furthering the readers' own fantasy lives. This publicizing of what has always been private may or may not be liberating or reassuring, but it is part of the inner experience writers' belief that it will be, and that "telling all" is a courageous project at a moral level.

However, if giving women access to their sisters' fantasies is a morally valuable goal, the contents of the fantasies must be liberated from moral judgments. Using Ms. Friday's own image, it appears that some people prefer hot fudge with their asparagus, but if that's what turns them on, it is by the logic of the image a matter of taste, not morals. Kinky fantasies do not indicate psychopathology (here Klinger and Singer would agree) and it is up to opponents of fantasy to demonstrate rather than assume harmful effects. Moreover, if fantasizing does enhance sexual pleasure and an open-minded attitude toward sexuality (goals many therapists have publicly endorsed), then it does seem that charges of escapism are misguided. Remembering that a philosophy of experience as a good thing in itself permeates the psychological literature, we can see how fantasy as a pleasure in itself could come to be valued and publicized.

Should anyone think that a better case can be made on behalf of fantasy by neglecting works like *My Secret Garden* and concentrating on examples of useful fantasy—exercises in therapy—we would argue otherwise. Many therapists will accept fantasy as a means to some other end, rather than as an end in itself. Nancy Friday's book makes fantasy itself and the pleasure it brings sufficient to justify rehabilitating it. Although at times one could argue that sexual pleasure is Ms. Friday's real goal, and fantasy a means to that end, there is another way of understanding the material she presents. For what most of the women daydreamers seem to want is not just physical pleasure, but entertainment. Some of the fantasies have a certain amount of intellectual elaboration, as did Walter Mitty's productions. Even if Ms. Friday herself created all the case histories, the element of entertaining-ness emerges (in some cases, the fantasies may entertain their creators but disgust or bore readers). Spontaneous fantasy, whether or not tied to sexuality, is the mind at play, losing itself in enjoyment of its own activity. To the Calvinist, this mental condition led directly to idolatry, a graver sin than lust. To the psychotherapist, still emerging from Calvin's heritage, fantasy must be justified by some effect or external benefit. But for genuine inner experience advocates such as Ms. Friday, fantasy is fundamentally its own reward.

Toward the Depths of the Soul, the Heights of the
Spirit

At the beginning of this chapter, we mentioned that religious visions of the past are not necessarily identical to
modern-day fantasy; so are the theories held today about
such experiences. Here is an example of a traditional
vision:

> Peter went up on the housetop to pray. . . . And he
> became hungry and desired something to eat; but
> while they were preparing it, he fell into a trance and
> saw the heaven opened, and something descending,
> like a great sheet, let down by the four corners upon
> the earth. In it were all kind of animals and reptiles
> and birds of the air. And there came a voice to him,
> "Rise, Peter, kill and eat." But Peter said, "No, Lord;
> for I have never eaten anything that is common or
> unclean." And the voice came to him again a second
> time, "What God has cleansed, you must not call com-
> mon." (Acts 10:9–16)

This passage from the Bible reveals assumptions fundamentally different from those of the psychological writers.
The author's interest was not in Peter's psychodynamics,
but in the abandonment of the Jewish dietary code, an
important decision affecting the Christian community.
The first assumption is that the true source of the vision
is God, not the visionary's creative imagination. Second,
the voice and the vision are as objectively real as the
housetop. Third, the vision is considered religiously authoritative for the entire community (not for Peter alone).
Any theory which assumes from the outset that visionary
experience can originate only within the self and can be
meaningful only to the individual experiencer will be at
odds with traditional religious assumptions on these basic
points.

It is the central core of Jung's theory of religion to identify a vision such as that attributed to Peter with contemporary experiences of waking fantasy ("active imagination" in Jung's terminology). Like dreams, waking fantasies come spontaneously and often without the consent of the rational ego. Sometimes there is a numinous sacred quality to their images, inspiring awe rather than mild pleasure or anxiety. This kind of fantasy experience may truly be called a waking dream since the alien and message-like qualities assigned to dreams from ancient times would also be appropriate to describe these experiences. Jung's writings on the spiritual meaning of alchemy draw interchangeably from dreams and waking fantasy. It is not possible to distinguish which productions are dreams and which are visions, especially since all of them are filled with exotic, archetypal symbolism. For instance, here is a waking dream which Jung considered extremely significant:

THE VISION OF THE WORLD CLOCK

There is a vertical and a horizontal circle, having a common center. This is the world clock. It is supported by the black bird.

The vertical circle is a blue disc with a white border divided into $4 \times 8 = 32$ partitions. A pointer rotates upon it.

The horizontal circle consists of four colors. On it stand four little men with pendulums, and round about it is laid the ring that was once dark and is now golden. . . .

The "clock" has 3 rhythms or pulses:
1. The small pulse: the pointer on the blue vertical disc advances by 1/32.
2. The middle pulse: one complete revolution of the pointer. At the same time the horizontal circle advances by 1/32.
3. The great pulse: 32 middle pulses are equal to one revolution of the golden ring.[18]

Jung comments that "this remarkable vision made a deep and lasting impression on the dreamer, an impression of 'the most sublime harmony' as he himself put it."[19]

It is this kind of waking fantasy which does start to seem comparable to Peter's vision. Another example, with symbolism much less obscure, also "came" as a powerful spontaneous vision:

DARK SHORE

There is a still, dark lagoon. The water barely ripples as I stand in a tiny boat and pole to the shore. Close by, a half-sunken large wooden vessel rests in the water, turned on its side.

I come to land. On the shore stands a tall, very thin figure wrapped in a robe, waiting for me. He has huge black-feathered wings. He stands expressionless, gazing out across the water.

I kneel down before him, kissing the ground in front of his feet. Then I say, steadily and trying to meet his eyes, "Sir, I had hoped that you would be more kind."

Without a reply, he leads me across to the island, until we come to a spot overlooking the water. I am left alone, to sit until the wind, bit by bit, blows me away.[20]

Within the context of Jungian thinking, to label such experiences "waking fantasy" is not to rob them of their religious significance but to raise them to the level of revelation, the encounter with an Other, or a force mysteriously working within the depths of the soul. The impact of such experiences can often be deep and lasting precisely because they are so different from the more typical mind-at-play kinds of fantasizing. Less cautious Jungians, and advocates of visual fantasy have gone on to equate such experiences with the visions of yogis and saints in the past.

It is at this point that the initial confrontation between

the Calvinist ethic of vigilance over mental life and pleas for fantasy takes on a new significance. For Nancy Friday, liberation from a puritan emphasis on real sex only meant freedom to enjoy fantasy experience, but was not construed as a religious challenge. But if one accepts the Jungian view, then what Calvin called the vast bubbling spring of the human mind is the locus of religious truth, and not primarily a source of error and idolatry. As Jung's followers have restated and refined this position, respect for fantasy implies an appreciation of religious polytheism (the "immense crowd of gods" flowing forth from the mind) and a repudiation of monotheism, particularly in its Protestant form.[21] The idolatry condemned by monotheistic traditions is reappraised as a path toward a new religious consciousness, one which acknowledges multiple powers at work within the soul. And no longer should vigilance over the mind be recommended but, rather, an attitude of trustful receptivity to its images.

If some waking fantasy can be a source of genuine—not idolatrous—religious revelation, then all fantasy deserves the benefit of the doubt. James Hillman, the most eloquent and consistent on this issue, argues against guided imagery techniques as well as Protestant monotheism when he decries them for their "abuse of the soul's first freedom—the freedom to imagine. . . . The autonomy of fantasy is the soul's last refuge of dignity, its guarantor against all oppressions."[22] As with dreams, the spontaneity and effortless quality of fantasy is transformed into a signal of spiritual freedom, the transcendence of environmental control. Hillman continues, "If we are willing to accept internal controls upon the imagination, we will have succumbed already in soul to the same authoritarianism that would dominate the body politic."[23] Once again, liberation through inner experience is liberation from an oppressive, inauthentic social reality, a liberation toward an inwardness which is religious and not merely psychological. Christianity is assimilated into the oppressive environment as a tradition which enforced internal control and condemned the visions of the soul as idolatrous. At heart, to choose in favor of inner experience is to set oneself against not just second hand religion but the entire Western monotheistic tradition.

Yet the same questions we asked about the liberating potential of dreams also apply here. Would Walter Mitty or Nancy Friday notice if Nazis were to take over their home towns? Would they be able to resist? Moreover, only in a very affluent society does the metaphor of hollandaise with one's asparagus ring true and to define one's human possibilities through this image reveals a shallowness in one's conception of freedom. Does the spontaneity of fantasy signify freedom or enslavement to one's self-deceptive ballistic mentations? Calvin did not trust the minds of men; Jung, Hillman, Singer, and Friday do, and must in order to make their cases. This trust is a matter of faith, a faith whose religious dimensions we are just beginning to explore. As we shall see, its polytheism is less apparent in relation to other inner experiences, but its emphasis on divine immanence, the within-ness of ultimate reality rather than its beyond-ness, is a continuous theme.

4

Mystical Experience: The Core of Religion

We are about to enter a domain of inner experiencing which is less familiar to most of us than dreams and daydreams. Mystical experiences have intrigued some psychologists and force inner experience advocates to confront the question of religion, its essence and value. In this chapter, we will examine their understandings of both mystical experience and its tie to religion.

"Have you had a mystical experience?" is not as straightforward a question as "Do you dream?" In order to answer the first, one needs to be familiar with some of the defining characteristics of "mystical," even at a rudimentary level. What characterizes most recent psychological literature is confidence in a certain definition of the mystical state, and overall agreement that this experience is by no means so rare and exotic as was once believed. Mystical states are referred to in passing in popular writings on other experiences, so that even when writing on dreams, an author will describe a state in which

our sensory, linear, time-space restrictions . . . are
transcended . . . everything is happening at once, as
countless strands of reality interpenetrate each other.
. . . The diaphanous film manufactured by our limited
awareness or self-knowledge is all that separates or
acts as a trap door preventing access to "deeper" levels of the Self.[1]

This level is assumed to be the referent for terms such as
Being, God, All That Is, and the Universal Mind. And this
assumption introduces a major motif of all modern psychological writings on mystical experience—its transpersonal, and thus transcultural nature. Mystical experiences
transcend ordinary culture-bound perceptions, and unlike
religious rituals, myths, or doctrines, are genuinely universal, panhuman. In the words of Maslow, the outstanding advocate for such experiences, they can become

a meeting ground not only . . . for Christians and Jews
and Mohammedans but also for priests and atheists,
for communists and anti-communists, for conserva-
tives and liberals, for artists and scientists, for men
and for women, and for different constitutional
types.[2]

Just as we know now that we live in one world, and that
the human race is one, so a religiousness rooted in mystical experience will be one, wherever it may be found. The
incipient polytheism of some advocates of fantasy is here
drowned out by an overwhelming emphasis on unity, the
oneness of All That Is and all authentic mystical religion.

But in order to reach Maslow's ideal meeting ground,
mystical experience must be considered in a certain way.
It must be defined as an experience which possesses certain qualities or earmarks, whatever the particular theological content of the experience. Of these qualities, the
most important is a sense of union or wholeness, whether
this is described by the experiencer in secular language or

as union with God. One experiencer might draw on scientific terminology, as in the following account of a mystical experience by the seashore:

> I noticed I was part of the same entity the ocean is part of. . . . I blended in, my molecules the same as Ocean's . . . just in a different structure, DNA sending my molecules different messages. . . . I was inside of whatever Oceana was also inside; me and the sea, mutual life. . . . There was nothing in that experience to deny or even diminish my individuality; instead, I began to perceive myself as part of a whole.[3]

However this sense of union is expressed, within whatever cultural framework, to psychological writers on mysticism it seems to be the most prominent feature of such experiences.

Other qualities considered among the earmarks of mystical consciousness are ineffability and the transcendence of ordinary space and time. Ineffable means beyond words, beyond all possible adequate expression. For the psychological advocates of mystical states such as Maslow, words were merely "culture-bound," and so the ineffability of mystical experience was a kind of proof for its transcendence of culture as well as conceptual thought. As for the sense of being "outside space and time," this too is well attested in the accounts given by and of experiencers. "The largest thing that had ever happened to her had, apparently, found room for itself in a moment of time too short to be called time at all."[4] In some psychological writings, the mystic's sense of transcending space and time is given plausibility through comparisons with contemporary physics. Here, neither space nor time as we ordinarily experience them are attributes of the ultimate structure of the universe. The mystic, too, it is suggested, has abandoned those familiar categories by which most of us live.[5] Real knowledge of All That Is is being communicated through the experience. As we shall see, this noetic dimension to the experience has caused problems for psychologists sympathetic to mystical states and anxious to advocate them. If "real knowledge" comes through the experience, how does one account for the very different claims made by Christians and Jews, atheists, scientists, and artists, etc.?

All of these defining criteria were set forth by W. I. Stace, a philosopher who believed that there was a core mystical experience which could be extracted from all particular religious creeds and contexts. Stace did make a distinction between "extrovertive" and "introvertive" experiences; the seashore example would be extrovertive, whereas in introvertive mysticism all external perceptions are transcended, and introvertive mystical awareness "has no content except itself."[6] This distinction has not proven interesting to most psychological researchers on mysticism, although it may be one way to distinguish higher, more rarefied states from more ordinary nature-mysticism. The rest of Stace's criteria proved appealing and adaptable to questionnaires and an overall humanistic setting. Stace's perspective on mysticism became taken for granted by many disputants during the 1960's controversies over the capacity of LSD to unlock a potential for mystical states. It was incorporated directly into Pahnke's research with LSD and "experimental mysticism."[7] Maslow elaborated Stace's criteria when he wrote about "peak-experience," a term which he used synonymously with "mystical experience" and "Being-cognition."

One of the great appeals of Stace's qualities, and the kind of approach to mystical experience they promote, is their alleged freedom from particular religious formulas. For instance, Stace proceeded by setting passages from Western mystics side by side with quotes from Buddhist and Hindu sources. Even the following example, from an Eskimo shaman, could be considered mystical:

I felt a great, inexplicable joy, a joy so powerful that
I could not restrain it but had to break into song, a
mighty song with room for only one word: joy, joy!
... and then in the midst of such a fit of mysterious
and overwhelming delight I became a shaman, not
knowing myself how it came about. . . . I had gained
my enlightenment, the shaman's light of brain and
body.[8]

The theological content of each experience can be set
aside: the Western mystic's interest in the Trinity, the Buddhist's in Nirvana, the Eskimo's in helpful animal spirits
are all localisms, or extraneous to the experience itself. At
least, this is the position Stace, Maslow, and many contemporary advocates of such experiences would take, which is
why it doesn't matter to them if individual experiencers
talk of God or Universal Mind or use language borrowed
from physics.

As we shall see, the supposed theology-neutral approach
to mystical states is by no means value free or even as
religiously universal as it claims to be. Moreover, advocating religious experience without advocating any particular kind of religion may reflect a broader American habit
of advocating religion in general, at the expense of all
particular religions and their interests. What contemporary advocates of mysticism insist on is that mystical religiousness is not as limiting as traditional church religion,
and that one does not have to be a "professional mystic" in
order to experience the world mystically. Along with these
claims goes a democratizing of mystical experience,
which is no longer the possession of a privileged few, but
available to almost everyone. Although this has its positive side, the result is often an implicit reduction of all
religious experience, past and present, traditional and
nontraditional, to a lowest common denominator. Far
from leading to genuine respect for the famous mystics of
the past, this can diminish their spiritual accomplishment

to the size of an average research subject's or reader's
peak-experience.

THE IMPORT OF MYSTICAL EXPERIENCE

Psychological theories about mystical experience are attempts to explain what happens during the experience,
and what its effects might be. Since mystical experiencers
themselves have strong opinions about these matters, it is
interesting to compare their views with those of psychologists. The chief surprise is that at least some psychologists
parallel or even duplicate the claims of mystical experiencers, although purporting to give a scientific and
objective explanation of the experience. The exceptions to
this are Freudian accounts, which play such a minor role
in the contemporary literature that they are mentioned
only by way of contrast. This does not imply that psychologists all assent to the mystic's claim of having experienced
God. But as we saw, God is not, from the Stacian contemporary advocates' point of view, part of the essential core of
the mystical experience anyway. The feelings of union,
ineffability, etc., are what psychologists seek to explain.
What several psychological theorists do endorse is the famous statement by William Blake, "If the doors of perception were cleansed, everything would appear to man as it
is, infinite."

The most scientific formulation of this idea is from Arthur Deikman, who suggested that during mystical experience a process of "deautomatization" occurs. The ordinary cognitive schemas we use to interpret the world are
temporarily abolished, permitting "a gain in sensory in-
tensity and richness at the expense of abstract categoriza-
tion and differentiation."[9] In other words, the doors of perception are cleansed, and our ordinary culture-bound and
tradition-derived knowledge is replaced by something
truer and more immediate. But Deikman is reluctant to

claim that the mystic experiences the world directly; instead, one experiences one's own brain processes:

> If awareness were turned back upon itself . . . this fundamental homogeneity (unity) of perceived reality—the electrochemical activity—might itself be experienced as a truth about the outer world.[10]

Because the brain is one, unity is experienced by the mystic who then mistakenly attributes this to a noetic insight about the external world. Deikman never shows how anyone can have a direct perception of his/her own electrochemical brain activity, which seems more problematic than mystical claims about the oneness of the cosmos. But Deikman's theory is popular because he makes mystical experience the undoing of cultural conditioning, a freeing from all social contact.

An alternative theory, which also frees the mystic from culture, is the Freudian or Rankian view which "explains" the experience by the idea of "regression." The mystic's sense of union is really a reliving of infancy or a before-birth state of union with the mother. This idea need not be used to discredit mystical experience; indeed one advocate of the prenatal explanation, Stanislav Grof, is also a vigorous champion of mystical consciousness. Here, however, there is an additional assumption that an interior return to a preculture, presociety condition is powerfully therapeutic. The mystic is one born again insofar as he/she undergoes a profound spiritual renewal. Once again, the mystic's claim to have experienced ultimate reality is reinterpreted (although perhaps symbolically prenatal existence is a kind of ultimate or primordial reality for human beings).[11]

A third theory comes closer to being a direct restatement of the essential core of the experience itself. This is Maslow's view, which is that peak-experience is indeed the

cognition of Being rather than of brain processes or union
of embryo with mother. The peaker knows the world to be
one because the world really is one. What Maslow calls
"Being-values" are apprehended in the experience: truth,
wholeness, goodness, and so on, which are clearly meant
by him to indicate objective qualities in reality rather than
merely the values subjectively ascribed to it by mystics.
These values "supply us with a perfectly naturalistic variety of 'certainty,' of unity, of eternity, of universality."[12]
Maslow is thus faced with the same question which so
many mystics encounter: if this is the way the world really
is, then why don't most of us perceive it this way most of
the time? There is nothing at all modern about this question. Julian of Norwich heard the Lord say, "All will be
well, and all will be well, and every kind of thing will be
well," and wondered why sin existed. For her, as for Maslow, this is not a cut and dried philosophical dilemma; it
is a deeply personal awareness of the gulf between the
perfection of mystical vision and the evils and imperfec-
tions of ordinary existence.

Maslow's answer, and that of humanistic psychology as
a whole, has been to insist that whatever keeps us from
peak-experience is accidental, and can be overcome. Un-
healthiness and rigidity and ignorance are all correctable
conditions; deficiencies in personality may be prevalent
but can be transcended. Are these factors due to some pri-
mal flaw in human nature, similar to original sin in Christian theology? Absolutely not, for although peak-experience may never become our normal continuous mode of
consciousness, the values and view of reality apprehended
in Being-cognition may well become our normal perception. The self-actualized person is one for whom this has
happened, for whom peak-experience is not only more
frequent but better integrated into daily existence. Maslow's emphasis on the intrinsic goodness of human nature
and the accessibility of its higher reaches has persisted in
psychological advocacy of mystical states. "The diapha-

nous film manufactured by our limited awareness" is not an inaccurate image; certainly there is no room at all for some innate and very solid evil tendency within the person which deliberately turns him/her away from ultimate reality.

And yet, if we are all so close to Being-cognition, there must be some negative force at work keeping peak-experiences from being noticed or respected. This force, for Maslow, was society in the sense of organized bureaucratic institutions, along with a narrow materialistic rationalism. For Maslow, both organized religion and organized science were opponents of authentic mystical Being-cognition. The spirit of nineteenth century science reduced life to mechanical, value-free quantities. The whole aim of humanistic psychology is to restore both values and authentic experiencing to man, thus producing a fuller and higher view of human nature.

Maslow also saw in conventional religion the enemy of mystical experience. The rulers of religious bureaucracies, he speculated, are by nature "nonpeakers," rigid and power-hungry types who try to suppress peak-experience out of fear.[13] As we shall see, the ultimate religious import of mystical experience is that it renders religious organizations unnecessary. At another level, this portion of Maslow's theory reveals the tendency of even the most optimistic and humanistic theorist to discover "villains" (the nonpeakers) who are to blame for the repression of mystical experience in our culture.

TOWARD A MYSTICAL RELIGIOUSNESS

Advocates of mystical experience often slip into identifying mystical states with religious experience. Clearly, for many of Maslow's followers, the core religious experience is unitive, ineffable, joyous, etc., and other types of religious experience are assimilated into this one mystical pattern. This is not so farfetched, given Stace's very generalized definition-by-qualities. Perhaps almost any private intense religious experience (conversion, for example) is at least to some degree ineffable, noetic, sacred, and transcends space and time. Even if a sense of union is the principle feature of mystical consciousness, one can be more or less generous in perceiving this quality in accounts which speak of the experiencer feeling one with Christ, or part of the whole world. To some extent, Stace's list of qualities does not really separate mystical from other religious experiences, but serves as a (supposedly) theologically neutral entrée into religious experiences which are intense, joyous, and memorable.

In the eyes of Maslow and those following him, religion's core of truth comes from this mystical peak-experience. Other elements in religion are secondary. If not false, they are certainly misleading and culture-bound. Only the mystical state is truly transcendent, truly an apprehension of Being.

> Small wonder it is then that the mystic, trying to describe his experience, can do it only in a local, culture-bound, ignorance-bound, language-bound way, confusing his description of the experience with whatever explanation of it and phrasing of it is most readily available to him. . . .
>
> I have, therefore, paid no attention to these localisms, since they cancel one another out. I take the generalized peak-experience to be that which is common to all places and times.[14]

Armed with a generalized idea of what the core of religion is, Maslow pruned away all else. For Maslow the localisms represent mere confusion and cultural conditioning and, in themselves, are not religiously or psychologically interesting. This is an extreme position, but it is one favored by psychological advocates of mystical experience.

Is the real purpose of this view to construct a theory

proving that all religions begin from a mystical experience? Although Maslow provided such a theory, it is subordinate to the contemporary religious goal. Whatever religion's core was in the past, today and in the future it ought to be mystical experience. Since peak-experience is utterly individual and outside culture, society, and tradition, "Each 'peaker' discovers, develops, and retains his own religion."[15] Such a religion has no need or interest in organization, fixed doctrines or transmission of its insights to others—who can after all have peak-experiences of their own. What keeps it from utter idiosyncrasy is that all peak-experiences are cognitions of Being and thus universal in essence. Only the localisms have prevented most persons in the past from recognizing this universality. Claudio Naranjo poetically located such a spirituality by contrasting it with conventional, traditional religion:

> It is with this trans-religious domain, or whatever name we give to it, that today's man is increasingly concerned. Religion is in autumnal foliage. The domain we discuss is with the roots, or within the ripening seed, in which the tree both begins and ends.[16]

In a sense, the religion of the future will not be religion at all, but an utterly privatized, interiorized apprehension of a universal force or power. Neither rituals nor myths nor public worship will be intrinsic to this transreligious domain.

This vision is already being realized in much of the inner experience literature, whenever an experience is considered sacred (apart from any traditional references), or when a how-to-do-it writer hints that when one takes dreams or sexuality truly seriously, one may discover and experience that level which has been called God, Being, or All That Is. Intrinsic to these claims is an opposition to all notions of religion as tradition. First, because the mystical experience is perceived as originating within the individual at a level where society does not and cannot penetrate. Second, because the ineffability of the experience means that it is impossible to communicate without sacrificing its essence. Third, because institutions, the guardians of tradition, are usually controlled by nonpeakers anyway. With few changes or refinements, Maslow and his followers turned William James's dichotomy between "firsthand" and "traditional" religion into an argument for the elimination of the latter. Although many psychological writers do not bother attacking traditional religion, they assume with Naranjo that it is moribund, and its kernel of truth can be gained as readily, if not more readily, by those far outside it.

This understanding of religion, whatever its limitations, has some powerful sources of appeal. It continues the American Protestant pattern of despising mere doctrine and a religion of secondhand externality. It rather ironically perpetuates a suspicion of religious reflection and theology, also typically American. An even stronger appeal may be its convenience for the very many contemporary Americans who are not really secular in their ideology, but who are no longer committed to or involved with Christianity or Judaism. A religion centered on private mystical experience allows room for an acknowledgment of sacredness without the obligation of membership in an organization. Given the freedom with which many people who saw themselves as alienated from religion used terms like "sacred" when under the influence of LSD, it is possible that many such individuals are waiting for an opportunity to experience "religion" outside churches. Few Americans may be truly hostile to religiousness, or truly committed to the kind of scientific rationalism which Maslow saw as so influential.

Even more concretely, the very amorphousness of peak-experience makes it convenient as a center of spirituality. In order to undergo conversion, you must believe in human sinfulness and the need for a savior. To identify

the savior as Jesus Christ, you need to be at least ac-
quainted with the Bible and accept it as authoritative at
some level. As we have seen, mystical experience requires
no such convictions. It need not be defined theistically, it
certainly leads to an optimistic view of human potentials,
and it is virtually content-free as far as making any definite claims on the experiencer's belief system and life-
style. For instance, the monistic theme behind the Stace-
Maslow characterization of mystical experience can be
interpreted as: (1) pantheism: God and the cosmos are one;
(2) there is a universal mind or a hidden spiritual force
behind all physical things (perhaps adapting certain Eastern monistic formulations); and (3) the universe is one,
and I am a part of it, just as modern physics teaches. Or
the experiencers can remain more vague and simply say
that they experienced reality, which is beautiful, joyous,
ineffable, and sacred. None of these claims requires either
a public commitment or a definite change of behavior.
Although the aftereffects of the experience may be quite
positive, it is the experiencer who decides what these aftereffects should be, and it is up to the experiencer alone
to evaluate what the experience was worth.

A BRIEF CRITIQUE: MYSTICAL STATES AND INTERPRETATION

Since the Maslowian approach to mystical experience
has been popularized throughout the inner experience literature, a few pointed criticisms of it might be very helpful. Obviously, committed Jews, Christians, etc., will have
their own criticisms to make of what they must see as a
watering down of specific theological claims, as well as an
insistence on a naturalistic explanation of religion. Another kind of criticism comes from those who oppose the
democratizing of mysticism, and who would argue that
true mysticism is much rarer than Maslowian peak-
experience. For instance, advocates of many countercul-
tural forms of religion argue that although peak-experi-

ence is one level of a religious state, there are many higher levels which can be reached only by specialized training. Such training involves meditative practice, a certain amount of self-discipline, and adherence (usually) to some particular system or master who explains an entire spiritual path. Although the lower mystical states may be accessible to all, only the initiated can really hope to reach the rarer, higher, and ultimate levels of consciousness.

Inner experience advocates with their roots in psychology are ambivalent about this claim. Distrusting the idea of an external authority, the practice of using a traditional system as a guide bothers many of them, especially since most traditional systems demand giving up things. On the other hand, since Maslow "discovered" peak-experience, it may have become too democratized for some persons. Highly esoteric multileveled systems prevent this from happening. An example of such a system would be the Arica training described by John Lilly in *The Center of the Cyclone.*[17] To carry this argument one step further, a strong sense exists that the system itself should never become an absolute, and so Lilly abandoned Arica and went on to other things. A traditional, multileveled system is both aristocratic and culturally-transmitted—and whatever its advantages over the psychological approach, for today's inner experience advocates, these same features will be a source of suspicion.

A third kind of criticism is based on a close examination of the criteria which constitute the defining earmarks of mystical experiences. To what extent are they truly religiously neutral? To what extent do they remain with the given of the experience? Certainly, they eliminate a great deal. Many mystics report a sensation of beautiful light, either golden or pale blue, suffusing everything. Why is this not one of the criteria of mystical experience? Another sensation is of buoyancy, but this too was neglected by James, Stace, and Maslow. Stace categorically declared that "Visions and Voices are not Mystical Phenomena"[18] but it is hard to say why not—except that they are too weird to make the experience palatable to many modern persons. Moreover, most traditional and modern mystics would strongly object to an emphasis on an experience stripped of its particular religious contents, for these and not the subjective qualities cited by Stace provide the ultimate significance of the experience. Some mystics experience the Trinity; others receive information about the condition of souls in the astral realm. The specificity and content-laden features of mystical experience can be dismissed as localisms only by someone prepared in advance to reject the religious claims of mystics. In this regard, the best counterweight to the Maslowian position is provided by the writings of mystics themselves, who mix images and imageless experiences, themes of union and separation, visions and voices and dark nights of the soul, with blithe disregard for the psychologists' criteria.

What seems to have occurred in the definition of mysticism is a selection of what is religiously believable to the selectors, in this case James, Stace, and Maslow. Monism —that being is one—is acceptable, while a Trinitarian God, the astral realm, and so on are not. However, even the qualities of the experience are already interpretations of the experiencer and the theorist. Years ago, Leuba (a critic of James) pointed out that union already suggests that "the mystical experience points to, or signifies, a union of individual with someone or something else" rather than a "gradual disappearance of boundary lines." This Jamesian notion of union is "just as much an interpretation" as the claim "of the Salvation Army lassie that she has met Christ face-to-face."[19] More recently, Proudfoot and Shaver reviewed Pahnke's study of mystical experience and came to the same conclusion: "The study of such experiences in abstraction from the interpretations is not the study of the experience at all"[20] since an entirely amorphous experience requires an interpretation before it can become meaningful even to the experiencer. A third exponent of this view is Gershom Scholem, the scholar of Jewish mysticism, who notes the "determining role" played by whatever interpretive scheme—naturalistic or traditionally religious—in shaping the meaning of mystical experience.[21]

From these scholars, we might conclude that Maslow's own naturalistic religiousness preceded all investigations into peak-experiences, as did his beliefs about Being-values and self-actualization. With this interpretive framework, he was able to rediscover a mystical core-religious experience which bore witness to a view of reality. Only from this particular religious stance can he then determine which localisms in mystics' accounts are really localisms (of no religious value) and which are genuine insights into Being. Such a view of mystical experiences and their import intends to be naturalistic and culture-free, but it is in fact determined by very specific cultural beliefs which most psychologists share. Like eighteenth century quests for natural religion, humanistic psychological searching for a universal core to religion naïvely minimizes the role of culture in shaping all experience. But unlike the deists whose natural religion took the form of specific propositions, the advocates of mystical experience can offer what is fundamentally an amorphous sense of oneness between the self and the world. In a fragmented and alienating environment, this may be comforting, but is it enough to bear the enormous weight of the expectations placed upon it?

Madness: A Journey Through the Depths

In this chapter, we will examine an inner experience far more violent, extreme, and controversial than dreams, daydreams, or mystical states. While madness is not "encouraged" by the popular psychological writers who advocate and extol the other experiences we have examined, their abundant interest in experiential reports of madness seems to derive from the same concern for authentic, inward experiencing that we have already perceived in the other contexts.

THE MAD PERSON AS HERO

Up to this point, the advocacy of inner experience has been relatively innocuous. To show that dreams, etc. are important for personal enrichment and development is not to make a serious assault on the status quo. Advocacy of mystical states need not lead to radical opposition to organized religion, nor are contemporary champions of mystical religiousness likely to be punished by church or society for their views. Moreover, although many inner experience authors use language which suggests a self utterly alienated from social roles and desperately searching for an authentic core, case histories again and again illustrate successful middle-class persons overcoming career and marital difficulties and becoming more successful. The alienated language does not imply that the ideal is to abandon all one's social roles and seek salvation in extreme withdrawal into self. Nor does it suggest a commitment to institutional change, the gradual fading out of organized religions (as in the case of Maslow and his followers) notwithstanding.

But in this chapter, the alienated self, severed from all social roles and robbed of all but its inner experiences, takes center stage. The mad person, for contemporary inner experience advocates, becomes a supreme test case of whether salvation through inner experience is possible. The mad person is the one who can no longer rely on society for support, the one shunned, incarcerated, and victimized by society—through its agents, psychiatrists—and forced to draw exclusively on inner sources of strength. The mad person does what the dreamer, daydreamer, and mystic are all trying to do: escape a world of social conditioning and achieve a new identity grounded firmly on the self's own powers. The major differences between the mad person's use of inner experience and the other uses we have seen are that the former encounters real and terrifying opposition from society, and the inner experiences themselves are filled with pain and terror. In the literature we will examine in this chapter, a new and purified self can only emerge through suffering, a theme not found in the promises of how-to-do-it writers or Maslowian mysticism.

Advocacy of madness does not mean recommending schizophrenia, manic-depression, etc., as beneficial growth experiences which everyone should have. Only in the late 1960s, a time of intense social turmoil and bewilderment over the boundaries of normality, could anyone have made this claim or even appeared to be making it. For our purposes, to "advocate" madness means to attribute to it some positive function for the afflicted individuals, and potentially for those of us who are not mad but might learn something about ourselves through listening to their stories. As R. D. Laing, a strong spokesman for this view, put it: "Certain transcendental experiences seem to me to be the original wellspring of all religions. Some psychotic people have transcendental experiences."[1] If certain (not all) psychotic persons have firsthand religious experiences which are both authentic and constructive for them, then our usual definition of madness as "mental illness" must be incomplete. For some writers, it is grossly, totally wrong.

> There is no such thing as schizophrenia, not outside some psychiatrist's imagination. There is pain and people's odd convoluted ways of trying to survive in the world. That's real. Not mental illness.[2]

But even this claim is not necessary in order to draw attention to the experience of madness as an important human situation, one well worth attending to in a world unwilling to confront such experiences unless it can turn them into medical symptoms. Several ex-schizophrenics insist that they were sick with a disease, but also insist that what happened to them while suffering was humanly important enough to retell in autobiographical form. And, whatever the theory of "mental illness" and its origins, authors of such autobiographies tell how a fresh and truer self emerged out of ghastly suffering. Only when all previous identities were no longer valid, when one was a "mental patient" and no longer a human being in the eyes of the world, could an authentic, inner-grounded voice be heard. As the eloquent Lara Jefferson, a patient in a mental hospital when she wrote *These Are My Sisters,* stated:

When a soul sails out on that unmarked sea called
Madness they have gained release. . . . For what the
sane call "ruin"—because they do not know—those
who have experienced what I am speaking of, know
the wild hysteria of Madness means salvation. Release. Escape. Salvation from a much greater pain
than the stark pain of Madness. Escape—from that
which could not be endured. And that is why the Madness came. Deliverance: pure, simple deliverance.[3]

Madness here implies a commitment—however involuntary—to rely on one's inner world, when the outer world
and the previous externally-based self could no longer be
endured.

For Ms. Jefferson and the majority of patients and ex-
patients who have given us their own stories, madness is
not a glamorous or romantic experience. It is not revolutionary, is never to be deliberately emulated or cultivated,
and would not be joyous and delightful even if the setting
in which it occurred were humane and sympathetic. It is
only when the interest in madness as a source of private
creative renewal combines with an overall hostility to contemporary society that the mad person becomes transformed (or deformed) into a revolutionary hero. If one
believes passionately and absolutely that all of modern
society is wrong, then anyone who rejects or has been rejected by that society becomes at least potentially a model
to follow, a liberated person who ought, on moral grounds,
to be imitated. In a potential outgrowth of such thinking,
schizophrenic withdrawal becomes a state to aspire to, as
it apparently was in R. D. Laing's therapeutic community
for a while.[4] Or the mental patient becomes a victim of
society, side by side with other oppressed minorities
whose liberation movements serve as sources for language about repression and alienation. From both these
developments we can learn something about the evils of

society as it is, but little specifically about what it means to be mad.

Any attempt to view madness as an authentic and perhaps valuable experience always risks romanticizing the mad person, as well as villainizing the representatives of institutional psychiatry. Our own effort is no exception; the best way to protect against this tendency is to stick closely to what mad persons themselves have had to say. The late 1960s and early 1970s saw a great many autobiographical accounts by mental patients and ex-patients. In addition, the film *One Flew over the Cuckoo's Nest* presented the "revolutionary hero" viewpoint of madness at its least subtle level. Previous works—such as Hannah Green's *I Never Promised You a Rose Garden*—have told the story of psychosis from the inside, but have emphasized a cure by psychotherapy. In the newer books, and the older ones which were reissued, psychiatrists are sources of confusion and humiliation rather than help. In these narratives the mad person is totally alone; each individual's salvation depends on abandoning all previous dependencies, including the (culturally conditioned) trust in medical authority.

Due to the above, and the relentless honesty of the protagonists of these autobiographies, these people are heroes, even when they are not particularly heroic in their actions. They are not revolutionaries, and not all of them claim transcendental experiences. But they do claim to have done what the majority of inner experiencers do not dare to, or need to do: they have abandoned all for the sake of a very interior salvation. They do not absolve themselves from blame—even those who see themselves as victims of an evil system—but they do speak with some pride as ones who have gone down to Hell and emerged out of the depths to triumph over ruin. Whatever the literary quality of these peoples' narratives, their acknowledgment of pain and despair helps save the inner experience literature from the triviality of how-to-do-it tinkering, and from the banal optimism of Maslow's mystical peak-experience religiousness.

THE SETTING

> If the Devil himself had been commissioned to build a hospital facility, this is how he would have designed it.[5]

Autobiographies by mental patients and ex-patients have two purposes: to acquaint "sane" readers with the inner experience of being crazy, and to shock them into concern over the terrible conditions existing in mental hospitals. Undoubtedly, psychosis would not be fun, even under the very best conditions, but a large part of the grief suffered by its victims is due to the setting in which they are placed and the modes of treatment they receive. Nothing can surpass the harrowing descriptions by Ms. Jefferson and her fellow sufferers of their fate, except for narratives from ex-inmates of concentration camps. Historically, at least some of those who wrote autobiographies went on to devote the rest of their lives to working on behalf of mental patients; Clifford Beers and Anton Boisen gained their fame through this activity as well as through their writings. Even authors who accept a medical framework for their experiences, who believe that they suffer from an illness called schizophrenia, have plenty to say about ill-organized hospitals with ill-informed staff, who perform their duties in an atmosphere of oppressive dehumanization.

What is perhaps the most shocking is the continuity and consistency of these observations over several generations. Beers, whose book *A Mind That Found Itself* was first published in 1907, emphasizes physical brutality in his discussion of indifference to the rights and humanity of patients. Episodes of brutality also appear in Lara Jefferson's *These Are My Sisters* from the 1940s and in Janet Gotkin's account from the 1960s. Even when the main theme is of neglect and deception rather than out-and-out sadism, the portrait of life in a mental hospital remains remarkably consistent over a long period of time. Given the enormous changes in American society's attitudes about mental health and the many new treatments available today, something is clearly amiss. Either things have not changed as much as most of us would like to believe or the mental hospital's overall impact on patients dwarfs the specific improvements noticed by outsiders.

Ex-patients' critiques of their treatment find at least four targets. These are the hospital environment and the relationships it creates, overuse of medication, physical abuse of patients, and persistent deception regarding the nature of their treatment. All these and more are seen as outgrowths of the hospital setting itself. The only possible redress is behavior which is interpreted by the staff as "crazy," that is, part of the illness from which the patients suffer. There is little in this portrait of mental hospital life which can be attributed to the illness of the autobiographers. In 1973, a now famous study by D. L. Rosenham dramatically vindicated this portrait. "On Being Sane in Insane Places" reported how "sane" experimental subjects faked symptoms of mental illness and got themselves admitted to hospitals. Once inside, they ceased all faking and tried to behave normally. They were never detected by the staff as imposters, and when they were discharged (some not for months!) they were often labeled "schizophrenic in remission" rather than "cured." According to Rosenham, the hospital setting created "depersonalization, segregation, mortification and self-labelling."[6]

Rosenham's experiment also highlighted the second target of the ex-patients: the mystique of psychiatric expertise. Again and again ex-patients report how little the theories and jargon of their doctors seemed to help, and how readily the staff hid behind these theories rather than confront patients on a person-to-person basis. Although some ex-patients report incidents of genuine kindness by staff members, the overall picture of psychiatry within the mental hospital is dismal. Doctors are seen ordering patients into submission, playing on patients' fears of abandonment, and in general enjoying the incredible amount of power over their charges which the hospital environment permits. Even outside the mental hospital, psychiatrists are reported to have broken up happy marriages, robbed patients or their parents of thousands of dollars, or dangerously overmedicated patients, all in the name of "therapy," but really for their own power and greed. Some of these accounts are more bitter than others, but very few of the autobiographies have any respect for psychiatric theory, and most are dubious about the benefits of specific treatments (electroshock and drugs are no more universally despised or feared than psychoanalysis). The fact that hospital staffs could not distinguish one of Rosenham's pseudopatients from the truly mentally ill seems to bear out the ex-patients' suspicions of psychiatric expertise.

It should be mentioned, however, that many recovered ex-patients attribute their experiences to an illness of some kind and claim that drugs or megavitamins or electroshock did help cure them. For persons writing from this view, Freudian (and Laingian) ideas about mental illness and early childhood are just so much garbage. For other ex-patients, their experiences are due to problems of personal identity, but not the kind Freudian psychotherapy can help with. A few patients are convinced that mental illness is itself a figment of psychiatric imagination. In short, one cannot say that those who have experienced psychosis firsthand are any more certain or unanimous as to its cause than is contemporary psychiatry itself. However, they are more than willing to admit either ignorance or a multiplicity of factors. Perhaps their major criticism of medical experts is that the latter pretend to know.

What keeps these accounts—or most of them—from being mere diatribes of maltreatment by hospitals and doctors is the wider context in which the authors often place their own stories. Like the prophets of the Old Testament, they are ultimately indicting society for its indifference, hypocrisy, and refusal of responsibility. It is not evil doctors and attendants, but a society which is willing to let mental hospitals remain long, long after their dangers are well documented that is the real target of the ex-patients. Society shuns and fears madness, does not want anything to do with it, and so lets the psychiatric establishment take control over the whole issue. Lara Jefferson saw society as hypocritical: anxious to cure the mad by building hospitals, but unwilling to prevent madness by, for example, making sterilization possible for victims of syphilis and other hereditary disorders.

At another level, some autobiographies insist that not only the hospital, but the entire setting of contemporary culture helps to generate madness. This was Laing's point, but it need not be made in the service of revolutionary rhetoric. As Mark Vonnegut, a young ex-schizophrenic says,

If I had had a well-defined role in a stable culture, it might have been far simpler to sort things out. For a hippie, son of a counter-culture hero, B.A. in religion, genetic biochemical disposition to schizophrenia, setting up a commune in the wilds of British Columbia, things tended to run together.[7]

In one way or another most autobiographers recognize that whatever the personal and medical dimensions of their madness, it is not an isolated experience. Its setting includes not only the hellish hospital but the whole complex and very demanding cultural milieu to which advocates of dreams and other inner states are responding, and within which all of us must learn to live.

LIVING DEATH, NEW CREATION

In order to write a coherent, comprehensible narrative, one must no longer be in the midst of madness; thus the lack of bizarreness in the style of most published firsthand accounts of madness. The contents—remembered delusions, hallucinations, ideas—may include extremely bizarre materials, but the style of narration includes no schizophrenic word-salad or other oddities. In other words, from studying published autobiographies, one can discover what it was like for various individuals to "go crazy," but this is not the same as hearing or seeing mad persons directly. A genuine "schizophrenic communication" could not generate the sympathy which the published accounts by the ex-mad do, even if one could understand it. We are referring, here, to recently published after-the-fact accounts about madness, such as Mark Vonnegut's *Eden Express,* Janet and Paul Gotkin's *Too Much Anger, Too Many Tears,* and Mary Barnes' and Joe Berke's *Two Accounts of a Journey Through Madness.* There are older writings where it is unclear if the author had really "recovered." The autobiographical *Memoirs of My Nervous Illness* by Judge Daniel Paul Schreber would be an outstanding example; this kind of work was actually more interesting to psychiatrists (including Freud), and other theorists than the more popular "how I made it through insanity" narratives.

In this writer's nonmedical view, anyone who can construct a coherent account of "how I made it through insanity" is at least partially recovered, even if he writes from within the hospital ward. Even if one makes a distinction between the live individual doing the writing, and the hero-protagonist in the narrative of recovery, it seems that to communicate emotional realities intelligibly is impossible for truly psychotic persons. To borrow the expression used by one pair of authors, these are accounts of "journeys through" madness, not messages from those lost in it. Whether the author returned to madness (as some did), the narrative of ruin, suffering, and recovery remains powerful. From our perspective, therefore, that these accounts are mostly after the fact, retrospective descriptions should not be discounted, for so are virtually all accounts of dreams and mystical experiences.

R. D. Laing schematized "the schizophrenic experience" as "a voyage from outer to inner, from life to a kind of death" and "then subsequently a return voyage from inner to outer, from death to life . . . from a cosmic fetalization to an existential rebirth."[8] We have no idea how well this description corresponds to any general "schizophrenic experience" but it captures the movement of all the published autobiographies. The first stage is of removal from all previous external ties, usually symbolized by entering the hospital. Gradually the protagonists are plunged more and more completely into their own internal reality. In the process, the world itself becomes strange, very strange. Janet Gotkin, one of the most down-to-earth of the autobiographers, describes her experiences just before her suicide attempt. She stood in her kitchen and confronted the gray-faced elders who had been present more and more frequently of late. She asked them to leave, but they replied, "Why, you silly, ugly, frightened girl, this is our home now."[9] Another protagonist spent an agonized weekend vacation with his family, convinced that a Chicago gang was following him and listening to his every thought.[10]

When the old, ordinary taken-for-granted world which the protagonist once shared with others is gone, what remains? Ruin? Deliverance? For many of the ex-mad, the answer is simple: what has replaced the old world is Hell, the place of death and of utter despair.

There is a word—it means Locked Eyes, but it implies more—it's the word for sarcophagus. It meant that at certain times her vision reached only as far as the cover of her sarcophagus; that to herself, as to the dead, the world was the size of her own coffin.[11]

For Mary Barnes, her "down" experiences were of death, darkness, nothingness, as she lay for weeks without moving, talking, or feeding herself, withdrawn from the world yet intensely aware of it in a weird way, aware of the emotions of the persons coming to her. Hell is traditionally the place of complete separation from God and all that is good, of hopelessness and the kingdom of Death.

> How appalling it was when Earth seemed full of innumerable brick-makers, building the walls of hell and the ovens, then Earth was not a living creature but a body embalmed and sealed in a sarcophagus.[12]

Yet paradoxically, for many who have experienced this descent to "Hell," it was not the start of their illness but the beginning of recovery. As Mary Barnes put it, "The big muddle started before I was born"[13] and the whole of her "sane" life had been a staving-off of madness. Thus, the utter ruin of the acute psychosis, the truly "mad" period, was a kind of salvation for her as for Lara Jefferson. Mixed in with imagery of death and Hell is that of conception and birth:

> In my room I lay on the floor in blankets that I wet and wet. Feeling very bad, lying still in the warm wet, I would go to sleep. Also, after playing with my shit, I would sleep with it on me. When Ronnie came I showed him my painting in shit on the wall. A sperm, an ovum, a breast. The Cross-Eternity forever. Birth-Suck-Suffer-Space-Eternity.[14]

And so, at the heart of Hell, the mad person finds the beginning of something new: conception, creation, new birth. The narratives vary in describing this, some more mythological than others in their approach. Mary Barnes, a Roman Catholic and a patient of Laing's, was encouraged to transform her inner realities into art by painting the crucifixion.

I did, again and again. From crucifixion to resurrection. Going down and in, coming up and out. Being
recreated, being reformed.[15]

In Hannah Green's autobiographical novel, the turning
point is a dream, a dream in which a powerful hand
presses pieces of coal.

> There was a sense of weighing, crushing time. She
> seemed to feel the suffering of the coal with her own
> body.... At last she cried out to the hand, "Stop it! Will
> you never end it! Even a stone cannot bear to this
> limit . . . even a stone!"
> After what seemed like too long a time for anything
> molecular to endure, the torments in the fist relaxed.
> The fist turned slowly and very slowly opened.
> Diamonds, three of them.
> Three clear and brilliant diamonds, shot with light,
> lay in the good palm. A deep voice called to her,
> "Deborah!" and then, gently, "Deborah, this will be
> you."[16]

With or without this powerful imagery, the suffering
protagonist discovers some mysterious inner force which
says, "You are going to live. You are going to be whole."
The husband of Janet Gotkin (whose kitchen belonged to
the evil elders) reported very simply, "She had undergone
a mysterious and profound change. A knot of despair had
broken apart in her mind."[17] Perhaps to some of the mad,
this moment never comes, and they remain lost forever,
but for those who have recovered there is a point at which
all things are made new, the world and their own beings.

Up to this point, things have happened to the protagonist
—mostly terrifying, sometimes bizarre or beautiful. Madness is not a voluntary process, and Hell and death are
fates suffered rather than freely chosen. The turning point
in the narrative is signalled by imagery of new birth, but
also by the protagonist becoming a genuine agent, as in the
determination, "I am going to get out of the hospital."

Then comes the decision which is made by the protagonist, whose mind is no longer a dry beach or under the
influence of "something".[18] According to one interpretation, the chief theme of these autobiographies is that of
becoming an agent rather than a victim,[19] a theme which
reveals a clear continuity with the how-to-do-it literature
on dreaming. Perhaps this theme is important in light of
the overall hospital setting, which encourages passivity
and fatalism. Janet Gotkin's husband noticed that after
her transformation, "for the first time in ten years of psychiatric experience, she no longer felt comfortable in the
hospital."[20] Once the protagonist has found a mind which
is truly his or her own, and so can act as a self among other
selves, the return journey can be made. Literally, this can
mean a return from the hospital back to the world of family and job, which is where most of the autobiographies
end.

And what has been learned from this journey? Some
report having touched on a secret, holy reality, an ultimate
knowledge almost impossible to communicate.

> I had got an understanding of things which I'd been
> trying to understand for a long time. . . . I was more
> —more than I had always imagined myself, not just
> existing now, but I had existed from the very begin-
> ning . . . from the lowest form of life to the present
> time, and that that was the sum of my real experi-
> ences, and that what I was doing was experiencing
> them again.[21]

Or, in the case of Anton Boisen who later became a pioneer
in the pastoral counseling movement, his psychosis gave
him this mission:

> I found some sort of process of regeneration which
> could be used to save other people. I had, it seemed,
> broken an opening in the wall which separated medi-
> cine from religion.[22]

Not all or even the majority of ex-psychotics are so explicitly metaphysical. Although terms such as "salvation" and "deliverance" are frequent, often what is learned is expressed as knowledge of who they really are as individuals, knowledge of the meaning of their sufferings for their own being. But one and all they recognize that "to be me" is unique and priceless knowledge, worth all the suffering, for it is knowledge which no one can take away.

The kind of "me-ness" which these individuals have reached is worth pondering, and comparing to popular ideals of a successful personality. As we saw in the writings on dreams, and as we will find in popular accounts of other inner experiences, the person who has found his or her "True Self" is assumed to be autonomous, joyous, adventurous, and open to experiencing. The other side of the popular ideal (at its crassest) is "to ride high, to enjoy, not to have to pay a price," and "not to have to be a victim is the only way to live!" Less crassly, the ideal person is one who lives perpetually in touch with such mystical values as harmony, joy, unity, and beauty, who welcomes "direct experience" without fear and so is able to see pain and evil as ultimately unreal. This is what William James called "healthy-mindedness" and it is certainly intrinsic to the magical hopes fostered by some how-to-do-it authors. But if we wonder if it is possible to live by riding high and not having to pay a price, the ex-mad person is certain that this goal is pure delusion, a delusion shared by most of American society but false to the core nevertheless.

After her recovery, Janet Gotkin acknowledged

> There has been despair. . . . That is part of our condition, to feel despair. That is what I am feeling and it is black and it wells up inside until you feel that you will explode with the heaviness of this sense of yourself, alone, in this unfeeling darkness that can be called the world. . . .
>
> Normal people did not want to die, they taught us; normal people never wanted to hurt themselves. That

> was sick. . . . No wonder I knew, inarticulately, that I
> would never be normal. I had touched these incalcu-
> lable wells of melancholy in myself and I knew that
> nothing could ever make them go away.[23]

Even if despair, pain, and melancholy are not the whole
of our condition as human beings, they are intrinsic to it.
They are not mental illness or some problems which will
go away. They are not removable by self-help tinkering,
and we cannot reprogram ourselves into not paying their
price. The essential optimism of "how I made it through
madness" is always qualified by similar visions of the
nonaccidental nature of suffering. For only the self discovered through the wells of melancholy can be real and
trustworthy.

A RELIGIOUS DIMENSION TO MADNESS?

One of Laing's key claims was that some psychotic persons have "transcendental experiences," experiences of a
universal, cosmic reality which are the very stuff of all
religions. Transcendental experiences as Laing defined
them are mystical; they liberate the individual from the
bonds of culture and the false, culturally imposed self, just
as Maslow and others claimed that mystical states do.
Laing insists that in a world utterly out of contact with its
own heart and soul, the mad person's experiences can
have a healing significance beyond the return to everyday
life.

> When a person goes mad, a profound transposition of
> his place in relation to all domains of being occurs.
> His center of experience moves from ego to self. Mun-
> dane time becomes merely anecdotal, only the eter-
> nal matters. The madman is, however, confused. He
> muddles ego with self, inner with outer, natural and
> supernatural. Nevertheless, he can often be to us,

even through his profound wretchedness and disintegration, the hierophant of the sacred.[24]

To be a hierophant of the sacred means to be a guide to realms of religious reality suppressed (supposedly) by our secular-scientific, "normal" culture. Madness is thus an initiation, a "breakthrough" (to a higher knowledge) rather than a "breakdown."

As we have seen, many inner experience writers are eager for a taste of this transcendental realm. For most of them, however, it is far more accessible, and the experience involves no total disruption of all previous ego-identities. Laing, however, has a much more critical stance toward contemporary society than almost all popular writers, so that one would almost require condemnation by that society in order to come close to transcendental truth. However, an alternative view is that whatever transcendental realities possess some mad persons, they are more profound and more powerful than what were described as mystical states in the previous chapter. Ordinary people, even in an inauthentic world, may have brief moments of Being-cognition but these will honestly not amount to much. The kind of inner journey which Laing attributes to the mad is much more extensive, transformative, and closer to the source of religious wisdom. It is involuntary; one is chosen for it by God or gods. It can be advocated, respected, and encouraged, but not tinkered into happening. Laing is not the only psychiatrist to have seen the mad person as engaged in some positive spiritual venture; John Weir Perry[25] and Roberto Assagioli[26] also claim this, although none of them maintains that all psychotic persons are in this category.

What about the ex-mad themselves? Do they see their illness as a spiritual quest, whether or not they use Laing's exact language?

For some, the answer is that Laing's whole theological interpretation of madness is irrelevant, for what matters is that they survived it, and are living more sanely and more happily than before their hospitalizations. They do not care to be "hierophants of the sacred"; yet even these would feel that in some way their madness was necessary for their inner development as human beings.

For others who have gone "through" madness, Laing's paradigm seems to fit; their madness was spiritual rebirth and they describe it in those terms. Yet the autobiographers are consistently more cautious about advertising themselves as hierophants, as misunderstood visionaries, than any theorist. For instance, Mark Vonnegut is familiar with Laingian psychology and rejects it because he believes schizophrenia is a disease and not primarily a transcendental state. But part of his madness was the culmination of a long-term religious quest:

> I thought about the things I had studied in religion, and about how much more of it seemed to make sense now. I had somehow touched what Jesus, Buddha and others had been talking about. . . . I became aware of a harmony and wholeness to life that had previously eluded me. Disconnectedness was very clearly illusory.[27]

And he admits that

> Everything I did, felt and said had an awesome grace, symmetry, and perfection to it. My appreciation of that grace, symmetry and perfection hasn't vanished with the insanity itself.[28]

Vonnegut, like Anton Boisen much earlier, had been fascinated by religious questions long before he became overtly psychotic. *The Eden Express* of his autobiography's title (taken from the folksong "This Train is Bound for Glory") is the symbol for his elusive spiritual goal, a goal he believes to have been shared by many of his generation. Is the entire move to avoid traditional, secondhand religiousness and go directly to the wellsprings and core of all religion an ideal not so different from the mad youth's? If so, then some mad persons are far more aware of the dangers of the quest than many of the normal who advocate it enthusiastically.

We have not focused on the many parallels which might be drawn between the mad person's death-and-rebirth narratives and the Christian passion story, or with initiation scenario and shamanic visions from all over the world. Such parallels could be used to show that shamans and visionaries are really schizophrenics,[29] or that there is one transcendental quest which all cultures but our own have valued. Which approach one takes depends on cultural and religious orientation. Perhaps to some extent the Christian model of death, descent into Hell, and resurrection has shaped the autobiographical narratives, given them a structure which their authors use for making sense of their own life histories. Although only a few deliberately use the crucifixion and resurrection theme self-consciously, others may unwittingly be guided by it. Certainly, these traditional themes provide vivid symbolism for the mad person to use. Once again, it is exactly at this point where religious commitment to an accessible monistic unity and benign harmony seems most inadequate, most unable to meet the needs of those who have gone to the depths and emerged through them.

6

Orgasm: The Liberation of the Body

Since our topic is inner experience, we will examine the application of inner experience advocacy to sexuality. The most appropriate topic for such a discussion is orgasm: what it means to contemporary writers, and the views of sexuality they try to promulgate or refute. We shall concentrate mostly on woman's orgasm, which has a different social meaning than man's and which many writers feel they have recently personally discovered as an experience.

REDISCOVERING "DOWN THERE"

Surely a future age will marvel at the immense literature written over the last two decades on orgasm, literature replete with detailed descriptions of what it feels like and how to get it. One good reason for our attending to the topic is that so many first-person accounts exist. Compared to the psychological materials dealing with mystical states, for example, the sheer quantity of writings on sexuality is staggering. Books such as Masters and Johnson's

Human Sexual Response or Shere Hite's *The Hite Report*
were best-sellers, and widely known even by those who
haven't read them. The literature on sexuality is also more
popular, more directed to the mass market, than the literature on mysticism.

There is further good reason for including the material
on orgasm in a survey of inner-experience literature. Up
to now, the experiences we have examined have all been
spiritual in the traditional sense: not disembodied, but
described without reference to the body. "Within" meant
"within the mind." In the literature on sexuality, however, we confront a strong repudiation of this mentalistic
framework, which is sharply criticized by all writers and
usually associated specifically with Western religious
traditions. Although the tinkering attitude makes the
body our instrument to some degree, much of the literature extols body-wisdom of an immediate, ecstatic kind;
body knowledge can be direct, ineffable, and immediately trustworthy. Our own direct access to our body's responses is the key to overcoming cultural programming
of all kinds.

With this outlook, popular writers on sexuality focus on
the traditional split between mind (me) and body (not me)
which has dominated Western life. Feminist writers point
to the paradox of the Western woman: the body to which
she has been reduced, whose appearance is frequently her
obsession, is simultaneously her greatest source of self-
loathing. Women are, to use the blunt language of one
writer, "cunt negative." "Down there" for most women is
still a realm of mystery and odors rather than pride. The
sexual revolution, about which many writers are ambivalent, seemed to ask women to take pride in their ability to
be sexy for men, but not for their own self-approval. As we
shall see, this issue becomes a major one in the literature;
is orgasm a key to a "social role" or a symbol of authentic
and autonomous selfhood? Either way, orgasm is a symbol, and it is useless to deny that it has and does function

this way for many people. Even if one completely disagrees with this ideology and supports the position of Masters and Johnson that "A woman cannot be sexually emancipated without first becoming personally emancipated. If she is nothing to herself, she has nothing to give to anyone,"[1] it is impossible to ignore the prevalence of the other position. This, an initiation into an entire sense of oneself as female, makes orgasm central. In the words of one popular writer, for a "real woman,"

> orgasm is the culmination of her physical rapport with someone of the opposite sex. It is her personal *tour de force* and proof of her identity as woman.[2]

Although feminists have fought this, by insisting on every woman's right to orgasm, they have probably fostered the symbolic centrality of this experience for contemporary women and men.

In this chapter we will try to summarize the applications of the inner-experience belief system and ethic to sexuality—particularly female sexuality. It will become clear that orgasm is as much a religious experience as a physiological one, as spiritual for many writers as are mystical awareness and lucid dreams. Given the very long opposition between spirituality and sexuality in Western culture, we find this particularly striking. Although all the popular writers on sexuality advocate tinkering in the sense of experimenting with one's own sexual responses (with or without a partner) and some go considerably beyond this, many also celebrate sex as a great joy, both a pleasure in itself and for what it contributes to human life.

> Spiritually, for sexual intercourse to be the ultimate satisfaction, both partners need a personal relationship with their God. When this is so, their union is sacred and beautiful, and mysteriously the two blend perfectly into one.[3]

For one of the most liberated respondents of *The Hite Report*

> Orgasm is an explosion which clears my mind, a force collected from my entire body, revitalizing and inspiring—like becoming one with the rhythms that run the universe, like receiving a personal message that life is good and beautiful. . . .[4]

These two statements, however different, both affirm the joyous, ecstatic, and truly abundant quality of sexuality, a message which pervades contemporary literature in spite of the banal, pompous, and often dismally work oriented emphasis on technique.

It is almost obligatory that the humanistically inclined writer deplore the technological approach to sexuality, an approach which dominates popular literature. An ethic of openness and self-exploration easily slips into an unlimited expression of the tinkering attitude, where an endless series of step-by-step directions for a wide range of goals becomes the norm. The how-to-do-it books in this area claim to instruct on: how to drive your man wild in bed, how to masturbate, how to overcome sexual hang-ups, how to enjoy sex in groups, with same-sex partners, with your dog. Some of the goals appear less concrete, for example, how to become a liberated woman. But often these too are defined through a series of step-by-step exercises. For those who find the tinkering mentality distasteful in and of itself, the entire range of literature covering the above-mentioned experiences will be dehumanizing and repulsive, regardless of which situations are being programmed or reprogrammed. Very few writers, popular and medical, recognize the liabilities and limitations of this approach. In this chapter, we will finally have to come to terms with the immense cultural prestige of tinkering as an orientation toward the self.

PHYSIOLOGY AND PSYCHOLOGY OF WOMAN'S ORGASM

In order to discuss the meanings given by popular writers to orgasm, we must recall that scientific laboratory studies of this phenomenon are even more recent than laboratory studies of dreaming. The explosion of popular writings following Masters and Johnson's *Human Sexual Response*[5] (published in 1966) is understandable. The advice books written prior to that date (and many written afterward) simply lacked the physiological information which most of the newer literature considers fundamental. However Masters and Johnson's data is interpreted, the assumption is that any serious discussion of sexuality must ground itself on their findings, even if it is critical of their methods and ideas. There is a lot about orgasm in women which we don't know yet, including its biological function (there are a myriad of suggested possibilities). But, thanks to Masters and Johnson, here are some things which popular writers assume we do know about the physiology of orgasm:

1. There is a definite cycle of sexual response for both men and women: excitement, plateau, orgasm, resolution. Timing of these phases varies by individual and under different circumstances.

2. Orgasm involves contractions in the vagina and uterus at .8–second intervals. Women may experience anywhere from about three to fifteen contractions.

3. There is no fundamental physiological difference between vaginal and clitoral orgasms, or between orgasm through masturbation or during intercourse. Though the experienced differences are real, they are a result of emphasis and attention—and social meaning.

4. No matter how close a woman is to orgasm, removing the source of stimulation will prevent her from reaching it.

5. Women are capable of limitless multiple and successive orgasms. Masters and Johnson cite the figure of fifty in a one-hour session.

6. Orgasm is a brief experience; it generally lasts six to ten seconds.

These physiological findings are the starting point for evolutionary speculations, feminist polemics against Freud, and hundreds of self-help books, not to mention the whole new area of sex therapy. What one makes of them depends on one's cultural presuppositions and moral commitments. Is the fifty orgasms per hour figure woman's "natural potential" for orgasm, thwarted by patriarchal society? Or is it just a freak piece of data? Does the dependence of women on continuous stimulation all the way to climax mean that women need responsive, considerate men as partners, or should they do it themselves because of that fact? Does the physiological identity of all orgasms mean not only that Freud was wrong to separate vaginal (good) from clitoral (bad) but that any orgasm is good and that masturbation is just as valid an expression of sexuality as sex with a partner? As can be seen, the answers to these questions are not physiological but moral-psychological. The questions themselves depend on specific views of women and the human meaning of sexuality, neither of which is given by the data.

If one makes orgasm the starting point, this already generates a certain set of priorities and assumptions. Orgasm is an "I-me" kind of experience.[6] "A liberated orgasm is any orgasm you like, under any circumstances you find comfortable."[7] An unliberated orgasm is one which is valued for what it can prove to someone else—the man who wants points for giving "his" woman an orgasm. A faked orgasm is a fundamental untruth, a symbol of woman's betrayal of herself, and accommodation to powerlessness. A consequence of making orgasm paramount is that whatever gets you there could not be all bad, and is probably valid or at least useful. Obviously, were procreation taken as the central principle for interpreting and ordering sexuality (the traditional Western norm) masturbation and women's sexual climax would both be considered at the very best irrelevant and at worst dangerous distractions from the proper goal.

To discover the psychological meanings of orgasm, what it's like to have one, requires getting away from laboratory techniques and asking people. As with mystical states, first-person accounts are absolutely crucial to an adequate view of the experience, and the newer literature is replete with first-person accounts from orgasmic women. There is, however, one limitation to these reports. An old folk saying has it that "If you doubt whether or not you've had an orgasm, then you haven't." This would correspond to one of the basic tenets of inner experience advocacy: the indubitability, the immediate given-ness of the experience itself. Yet many women honestly do not know if they've orgasmed, or report that at one time they thought they did but later learned better. In other words, genuine mistakes about one's experiences are possible, and are admitted to be frequent by the more sophisticated writers. Feminists see this as a sign that women's basic relation to their own sexuality has been repressed and distorted by patriarchal culture. Some writers, therefore, feel called on to provide definitive, detailed clinical descriptions of all the sensations so that women will be able to tell for sure if they've had the experience.[8] These descriptions and others by women experiencers themselves are not meant to be read as works of literature, since they consist principally of endless near-clinical prose. The exception would be someone like the lively but not factually informative respondent who, when asked how she masturbated, replied, "I simply think locally stimulating thoughts, then a brief touch of fingers and it's over. Ha! Sneaky, isn't it!"[9]

The descriptions provided by women include all sorts of details about contractions, a feeling of stoppage or suspension before the contractions, and vaginal ache when orgasm occurs without penetration. There is a minimum of romantic "waves of ecstasy" language in many of these accounts. "It starts at the clitoris and surrounds the vagina like a hoop."[10]

> Orgasm starts as a pressure from within and a tingling tension near the clitoris, which spreads to the vagina inside my abdomen. There is a general stretching tension throughout until orgasm breaks.[11]

If the value of these reports is to compile a definite, widely accepted account of the exact sensations of the experience, then they have far more merit than the following:

> There is an almost frantic itch-pain-pleasure in my vagina and clitoral area that seems almost insatiable, it is also extremely hot and I lose control of everything. Then there is an explosion of unbelievable warmth and relief to the itch-pain-pleasure! It is really indescribable and what I've just written doesn't explain it at all!!![12]

> You feel it everywhere. You are not aware whether these extra-special orgasms are vaginal or clitoral. You even feel them in your scalp and the soles of your feet.[13]

Given a background belief that an important inner experience ought to be beyond all doubt, obviously and instantly recognizable for what it is, the importance of exact description—and of overcoming women's ignorance and confusion—is easily understandable. Even the clinically uninformative reports contribute to the overall sense of ultimacy and ecstasy surrounding this experience.

For some women, the contrast between clitoral and vaginal orgasms continues to be meaningful at the level of psychological experiencing. According to Dr. Seymour Fisher, "clitorally oriented" women tended to stress what he labels the "ecstatic" aspect of sex, while the "vaginally" oriented leaned toward an ideal of "fusion" with a partner.[14] There is nothing pathological in either mode of experiencing, but feminist writers clearly prefer the first for psychological reasons. Fusion with a man is not necessarily an unliberated goal, but it is, in the eyes of many writers, basically an imaginary one. While you are fusing, he may be thinking of anything, and Ms. Morgan's hope that "the two blend perfectly into one" will always be symbolic rather than literal. As one self-help manual revealingly puts it:

> Your sexual response is locked within your own body. Even during intercourse, male and female remain separated by the skin of the penis and the lining of the vagina. Just as you taste and digest your own food, so you take responsibility for your own orgasm.[15]

Note the jump from physiological fact to moral injunction; this is a common method of arguing.

The comparison with digestion makes clear what we have so far presupposed: orgasm for women is an internal experience. There are a few clinically observable signs that a woman has climaxed but that has not meant that women have stopped faking orgasms or that men can no longer be fooled. Given what one woman referred to as the "Orgasm Olympics," the enormous pressure put on today's women to perform spectacularly in bed, fakery has obvious benefits. Hite's collection of confessions on this point are pathetic and poignant evidence that the *Playboy* style of sexual revolution may have made things worse for women.[16] Few of the fakers gave as their reason any genuine concern for the man's feelings. The most prevalent answers were to avoid a fuss (due to low self-esteem) and to gain approval from a man. These are something like the reasons used for not attending to inner experiences such as dreams: social pressure, and a general lack of trust in one's own resources. Here, they serve to enhance the special power of what is already widely believed to be an "ultimate experience." This is not the same as unintentionally, inadvertently beefing up one's inner experience, of course, which is not considered a problem by inner experience advocates. There are, as we mentioned, women who are genuinely confused over whether they've orgasmed. But "faking an orgasm" is defined as just that. It is not unintentional, not innocent, and to many authors, women and men, it is a crime against one's own integrity. This too fits the overall moral theme of the inner experience literature: one either trusts one's own experiences—what one really does or doesn't feel—or one submits to the inauthentic, turning oneself over to the powers-that-be and to their ideas of what one ought to feel.

The internal nature of orgasm links it to dreams; its ecstasy to mystical states. But sexuality has been viewed in our culture as fundamentally social, a "we-situation" rather than an "I-me" experience. Until recently, the ideal sexual situation was considered one of I-thou sharing between two partners. Internal sensations were interpreted in the light of this mutuality—their "meaning" was viewed in a context of shared experiencing. This may have been the ideal, although in actual practice, feminist writers claim, the socializing of the sexual situation meant a power struggle where women "gave themselves" to men, or men "took" women. One way to overcome this is to reaffirm the ideal of mutuality between equals. Another way is to accept an unequal distribution of power, but emphasize the amount of covert power available to the woman through manipulation and bamboozlement of men. A third way is to redefine sexuality so that self-affirmation and autonomous ecstasy become keys. The third move all but assimilates sexual experience into mystical states and other inner experiences of the most private kind. It invokes an ethic of autonomy at which we have only hinted.

"FOR MYSELF": ORGASM AND AUTONOMY

One medical-advice book insisted "You must take responsibility for your own orgasm." It is impossible to overestimate the centrality of this theme in much of the newer
literature written for women. Not only is orgasm a symbol
of woman's own internal, natural potential for self-tran-
scendence, and self-affirmation, but the entire process of
achieving orgasm is now her responsibility. It is no longer
the man's duty to give her an orgasm (the Mr. Right view
debunked by Hite and others). Even if the importance of
the partner is recognized, it is the woman's responsibility
to inform him of her likes and dislikes and of what he's
doing right or wrong. But before she gets to this point, she
must take responsibility to pursue the quest for orgasm on
her own.

Because orgasm is presumed to be a goal which is worth
striving for, this language is fully appropriate. Naturally,
even the most radical feminists allow that occasionally
women and men may both want sexual contact without
orgasm. Physical and emotional closeness, intimate showing of affection; no one claims these are unworthy or
should not be part of sexual experience. But few of the
many books on sexual behavior for women would be written were these the main goals. Rather, orgasm is addressed as an extremely specific goal which can be ration-
ally, systematically pursued.

Most self-help writers suggest the following general program: first orgasm by yourself, then with a partner. It is
convenient to label the first situation masturbation, the
second intercourse. The advantage of masturbation as a
situation for learning about one's sexual response is that
the entire process is directly under one's own control. This
point is stressed by authors, whether they see orgasm by
oneself as a preparation for intercourse, or as a valid experience in itself. Because control and rational planning
often go together in Western society, writers who value

self-direction in sexual activity tend to accept a model of
technical productivity. If orgasm is the product, there
must be various steps and stages involved in its production. The person who wishes to take responsibility and
control over her own orgasm will follow the necessary
steps carefully, check thoroughly that each is mastered,
and view the process of becoming orgasmic as an extension of her rational capacity to exert control in solving a
difficult technical problem.

This model of action, imported from sequential industrial production, forms a backbone for specific advice and
techniques. For example, a manual on women's orgasm
offers an "Eleven-Step Program for Achieving Self-
Stimulated Orgasm" (followed by "Ten-Step Program for
Achieving Orgasm with Intercourse"). The methodical
authors begin from the beginning: Step 1 (Self-examina-
tion) and include exercises, autosuggestions, vibrators,
fantasies. If you are not orgasmic by Step 11, "possibly you
only followed the instructions half-heartedly and not very
conscientiously, in which case you could simply begin the
program over again."[17] A great deal of the inner experience literature may express disillusion with and alienation from technological rationality, but this mood does not
appear to have influenced writers such as these. When one
has already defined a complex human experience by isolating a specific goal, it is probably true that this pragmatic, small-steps method works better than any other.

But a very different approach toward rehabilitating
masturbation is recommended by Betty Dodson, in a really
original pamphlet entitled: *Liberating Masturbation: A
Meditation on Self-Love.* Here, the goal is broadly defined:
to get women to be "cunt positive," to affirm themselves
and their bodies. Orgasm is a key here, but it is in a context
of overall self-affirmation. Thus, rather than devising a
step-by-step program toward a narrowly-conceived goal,
Ms. Dodson asked women to draw each other's genitals—
"the Goddess emerging to take her place. . . . Now it was

not the male version of the cunt, the split beaver of the porn shops, but the woman's version of herself."[18] From this point of view, masturbation is no longer a preliminary practice for intercourse, but an experience of one's own autonomous potential for pleasure, and a sign that woman's overall identity can be for herself and independent of a man's presence.

It is here, of course, that those who emphasize feminine dependency part company from the more inner experience oriented authors. If an orgasm is primarily "proof of one's identity as a woman" to a man, then masturbation can never have more than a practice function. However, even a book by Joy Warren called *How to Be an Erotic Woman* (published by Award Books) which fully supports an ideal of woman as sex-object for men, allows the woman a great deal of autonomy and recommends a range of tinkerings which she initiates and controls. Bamboozling a man with gimmicks—from costumes and wigs to physiological tricks—implies that the woman has a range of options and is free to stage-manage sexual relations in a nontraditional fashion. It is perfectly true that such works turn sex into a performance, the woman into an object, and contribute nothing to the true goals of feminism. But as with a great deal of popular inner-experience literature, their principle theme is: don't be a victim anymore! You can be in control.

If this is the basic message of even the least liberated of the current literature, it is worth asking (as we did in the chapter on dreams) if freedom can be found through this kind of autonomy. After all, women have been preoccupied with their own sexuality for thousands of years. Politically oriented writers would see even the more creative expressions of the newer writings on feminine sexuality as a continuation of this narrow focus and a distraction from more significant economic and social struggles, which (they would say) are the more important shapers of women's possibilities for full humanity. But what of well-intentioned attempts to reintroduce an ideal of sexual mutuality, rather than autonomy? Are these naïve? Sexual relations in the past have not been based on mutuality; that ideal has not worked out in practice. The answer may be to decenter sexuality itself as a locus for identity-formation.

> It would be . . . more logical for a man or a woman who lacks a sense of self-esteem and who feels cheated of happiness to begin . . . by undertaking achievements in other aspects of their lives.[19]

MYSTICAL SEX

In the minds of most persons today, sex and religion are opposites. Western religious traditions have been blamed repeatedly for inducing and perpetuating ignorance, repression, guilt, and "demonization" of sexuality (particularly woman's sexuality). The opposition between a strict, repressive, religious upbringing and the discovery of one's own healthy sexuality is an underlying theme of first-person accounts and advice books. Repeatedly, to acknowledge and enjoy one's sexual energies is the sign of rejecting religion, for religion is equated with oppressive teachings on the sinfulness of the body, and massive guilt producing ignorance on the whole subject of sex.

If even half of these accounts were accurate, religion has clearly played a major role in ruining modern people's quest for natural enjoyment, in forbidding them to explore their inborn potential for orgasm.

The reason I say "if " is that there is some evidence that strictness of upbringing and religious training is unrelated to whether a woman is orgasmic.[20] Obviously many women who are unhappy about being nonorgasmic blame their backgrounds, including their religious instruction. But others from equally rigid backgrounds never had any more problems than the lusty lady who claimed:

> I don't think that what your parents or teachers do is that essential. If you're a fairly healthy young female animal and you chance across the right boys, you're going to be crazy about sex.[21]

It may not be that simple, but it appears that the opposition between traditional religion and the joy of orgasm should not be used as a primary explanation for why all women are not orgasmic.

What is the meaning, then, of all the fervent polemics *against* repressive religion? We believe that the current literature expresses another variant of James' opposition between conventional, traditional religion and real religion, rooted in intense inner experience. For many current writers, orgasm in particular and sexuality in general is a mystical, transcendent state, with all the possibilities for overcoming enculturation which Maslow perceived in peak-experience. As we have already seen, orgasm, like a mystical state, is ineffable and is a pure affirmation of energies in oneself and the universe.

> Anyone who has enjoyed sex at its finest will recognize that it can be, and is, an almost mystical experience of renewal, where body and soul seem to be perfectly integrated, existence is given meaning, and immortality is somehow affirmed.[22]

In spite of an overriding emphasis on autonomy, orgasm is an experience of ego loss for many and is treasured as such. It makes no difference that it may last for only ten seconds by the clock, any more than it would for the peak-experiencer.

This idea is a new one for most Westerners, and it is

certainly not one which traditional mystics would endorse. But at points it rescues contemporary literature on
sexuality from critics who would see all the materials we
have discussed here as representing only a search for
kicks and cheap thrills. Mystical orgasm is free, but it
becomes—or can become—a genuine way of restoring to
ourselves a more primordial harmony with the cosmos.

> It was ... a union of the most primitive state in which
> animals possessed nothing but touch to express their
> feelings, and the highest spiritual state in which lan-
> guage comes face to face with the infinite.[23]

Yet, to give critics their due, orgasm sometimes replaces,
in reductionist fashion, all other religious experience. For
example, one author claims it as "the most religious moment of our lives, of which all other mystical kicks are a
mere translation."[24] The claim that sexual experience can
be mystical may be an authentic expression of a spontaneous, joyful discovery, or it may be an endorsement of a
shallow hedonism.

The mystical nature of sexuality represents a genuine
twentieth-century discovery and a personal turning point
for many persons. The women subjects of Hite's *Report*
and those of some of the other studies have put up plaques
in their lives commemorating this sudden insight. For
them, it was often a real revelation that joy and pleasure
are accessible, given free to all, and abundantly stored in
our very flesh. In our view, this is a rich and exciting
discovery and represents a definite advance over traditional Western religious teachings about sexuality.

Finally, because this discovery is made in the context of
the same psychological, ethical, and spiritual claims
made on behalf of other inner experiences, it stands or
falls on many of the same grounds.

Dying: From Pragmatism to Transcendence

Until a few years ago, a common theme among many cultural critics was American society's repression of death and dying. Although this may still be the case, there is now a large body of writings, popular and scholarly, on the subject of dying. We will examine some of this material in this chapter (it is virtually impossible to cover all of it) and look especially at its underlying continuity with the rest of the inner experience literature.

The new literature on dying includes several classes of materials. We have clinical studies of the dying and the psychology of terminal illness, among which Elisabeth Kübler-Ross' *On Death and Dying* is by far the best known. There are how-to-do-it books written for the dying and their families, with titles like *Coming to Terms with Death* and *To Die with Style.* There are technical works in the field of medical ethics, and popularizations of this area such as Marya Mannes's *Last Rights.* Then there is another class of writings which offers detailed accounts of what the dying experience and which often imply an entirely different understanding of death than all of the

other materials. Raymond Moody's *Life After Life* is the
best known of this group. When we refer to the newer
literature on dying, it is to these various writings that we
will point.

These materials are contemporary in several senses.
What distinguishes all of them from most traditional cov-
erage of the subject is not new medical discoveries per se,
although some ethical questions (such as when to remove
a patient from a respirator) are clearly tied to contemporary medical techniques. This literature assumes a special
locale for dying: the modern hospital, which like any large
institution, will often subordinate human needs to
schedules and red tape. Contemporary writers are aware
that the practical issues facing the dying patients and
their relatives are a mixture of medical and psychological,
as well as economic. The hospital setting for dying also
raises questions about the involvement of children: should
they be told? be brought to visit a dying relative? To some
extent, today's works on dying can be distinguished from
all previous writings simply because they reflect the contemporary medical and social setting in which dying most
often occurs (today approximately eighty percent of
Americans die in hospitals).

But at a deeper level, these writings involve a far more
radical departure from past eras' treatments of the subject. They are resolutely secular, much more so than the
literature on sexuality. References to traditional religious
teachings and practices appear scattered throughout, but
are of little concern to most of the writers. The perspective
from which advice is given depends on a pragmatic and
almost utilitarian attitude toward the larger religious
questions raised by dying. Patients have all sorts of religious beliefs, which it is not the job of a psychological
counselor to undermine or criticize. But there is a tacit
assumption that these beliefs "work" only for a small
group of patients. The rest must either founder in mean-

inglessness, or be helped toward some secular framework for coming to terms with dying.

Our use of "secular" here is perhaps confusing. Surely *The Hite Report* is a secular book, even if many of the women surveyed found orgasm a mystical experience. Because this is true, it is also a good point of comparison. Orgasm is natural, but for at least some experiencers and popular writers, this means that it puts one directly in touch with the deepest and best forces in the universe, with cosmic rhythms and energies otherwise suppressed from our beings. Death, too, is "natural"; it happens to everyone, it is a biological process, etc. But in most of the contemporary literature on death, natural has no cosmic or ultimate dimension to it. Death simply happens and should be accepted. It is natural rather than supernatural, but not natural in the additional sense of liberating from cultural forms or transcending conditioning. (Not for most writers, anyway.) Ironically, exactly this aspect of death appealed to late Medieval thinkers who saw death as a great relativizer of social distinctions, the enemy of all pretensions to power or grandeur. This idea, with its revolutionary undertones, plays no role in the contemporary literature. In fact, by calling the latter "secular," we mean to imply not only the absence of religious language, traditional and otherwise, but the flattening and narrowing of the discussion to exclude any explicit references to an ultimate or cosmic dimension of existence.

Not all newer writings share this quality, but the majority are amazingly narrow in their pragmatic approach. Death is something we don't understand and can't do anything about. Dying, on the other hand, can be studied and with proper understanding can be transformed into a positive experience, or at any rate become much less of a horror than it is for most Americans. Even if the medical prognosis is fixed, what can be changed is one's attitude toward one's own demise, and this is the focus of the vast majority of how-to-do-it writings. But there is something paradoxical in this (although such an approach can be helpful); the dying patients are often explicitly exploring the larger, philosophical questions which many of the psychological writings hope to ignore. In a study where the psychologists themselves were interested in philosophical and religious dimensions of dying[1] their subjects' own religious reflections were given some space. It seems, though, that the closer a writer gets to the day-to-day life experiences of hospitalized, terminally ill patients, the more the philosophical-religious questions are laid aside.

One reason for the pervasive secularity of most of this literature is that it is deliberately aimed at a wide variety of readers from all sorts of backgrounds and with diverse convictions. Religions have specific and sometimes very detailed teachings about death, whether these are accepted or even understood by all believers. Because the traditional teachings about death are well known, a psychological writer trying to be helpful will not begin with a diatribe or an attack on religious views of heaven and hell—not unless he or she wants to offend a good percentage of the readers. Although it may become clear that the how-to-do-it writer's own convictions are quite different from traditional ones, each will focus on matters which are less problematic, such as the dying person's right to express his or her own feelings and thoughts to a sympathetic person. Therefore, in the eyes of popular writers, religious views remain a matter of individual options and choice, dependent on one's previous commitments, while the psychologist's advising is perceived as more inclusive, as relevant for Christians, Jews, atheists, and their families. Here, once again, psychology claims for itself a universalism as opposed to the particularity of religious traditions. Dying as inner experience includes everybody; death as a religious event, or debates over an afterlife, concern only some persons.

Another theme unites the literature on dying with the

writings on dreams: the notion that in the past the experience was given more respect, and more adequately handled. The contemporary interest in dying is a rediscovery of what most peoples all over the world knew, but what modern Americans have forgotten. As with dreams, it makes no difference that in the past the experience was always given a religious interpretation. It was taken seriously, and not repressed or denied. Even if people everywhere always feared death, they knew how to make dying an integral part of living, and how to handle grief and mourning without psychologically isolating those most affected, some of the skills newer literature tries to recover. For example, Kübler-Ross' famous *On Death and Dying* begins with a traditional deathbed scene recalled from her Swiss childhood.[2] In the words of Philippe Ariès, death throughout most of human history was "tamed." "I do not mean that death had once been wild and that it had ceased to be so. I mean, on the contrary, that today it has become wild."[3]

DYING AS INNER EXPERIENCE

We will begin this section with the reflections of a terminally ill man.

I don't think anybody wants to die. It really wouldn't bother me that much, like I say, but I think of all the . . . different things that I'll be missing out on as far as my family is . . . my family, goes, you know? Like my children's graduation and weddings, and grandchildren and all. This is something I've looked forward to, grandchildren, for years, you know. . . . So naturally I'd rather live until I was seventy-five, that's all. But like I say, it isn't what I'd rather do; that's not what the deal is here. Life is like a trip to the store, you know. Your mother sends you to the store for a loaf of bread or something, in other words that's how

fast it goes. In ten minutes it's over and you're back
and I compare this life . . . this average sixty-five,
seventy years to a ten-minute trip to the store. . . . It's
really not that important.[4]

To grasp dying as a human experience implies attending to thoughts like these. They are a primary source of
data for contemporary psychologies of dying and grief. By
psychologies we mean no elaborate theory such as Freud's,
but a simple schema or pattern to order the diverse
phenomena experienced by the dying and those who help
them. Such a schema is Dr. Elisabeth Kübler-Ross' five
stages, explained in *On Death and Dying,*[5] and copied and
publicized in an enormous number of writings. There is
not really much experimental evidence to support the five
stages but due to the simplicity, utility, and implicit moral
values of Kübler-Ross' stages, this pattern is widely accepted in spite of a minimum of objective evidence to support its veracity.

At the heart of Kübler-Ross' idea is the belief that dying
can be understood as a systematic, internally-coherent
psychological process. Even if it is not always experienced
in this way, a strong implication exists of a natural progression from denial to acceptance, an implication tied to
the term "stages." This implication dovetails with how-to-
do-it thinking, i.e., if there is a progression from *a* to *z*,
then there must be guidelines or techniques to make the
progression quicker or less painful, or to hurry through
the intermediate *b* and *c* stages. This was not Kübler-Ross'
intention when she developed the scheme of five stages,
but it is a problem endemic to any notion of "progression"
suggested within a society open to tinkering. In Kübler-
Ross' own work, the stages seem to represent five attitudes
which do not, in many cases, follow one another in clear
sequence. In a taped interview watched by this writer, an
elderly man with cancer, in the course of a ten minute
conversation, expressed typical feelings associated with

all five stages. Obviously, one is talking more about a way to classify divergent attitudes (in this case all coexisting) than about a linear progression.

The simplicity and beauty of Kübler-Ross' scheme is that it does classify almost all possible expressions of feeling under five different headings: denial, anger, bargaining, depression, acceptance. These labels do seem to suggest a progression with respect to the desired outcome—an acceptance of what cannot be changed. An additional reason for the popularity of the Kübler-Ross' scheme is that it can be applied to the psychology of mourning as well as dying; it is a system for making sense of human responses to any situation of loss or grief. It has probably helped create an ideal pattern, or given voice to an implicit ideal, and is thus incredibly valuable. There may be many phenomena not covered by this scheme, and some parts of it, such as bargaining, may be elusive and all but impossible to research using ordinary methods. But these five stages form the backbone for most of the newer popular literature, and for widespread public interest in helping dying persons as human individuals rather than as medical cases.

Kübler-Ross' work takes the hospital setting as the norm. Here, we find patients who are not on the brink of death but who suffer from terminal illnesses, lie in bed, or sit in lounges away from home, surrounded by strangers and strange equipment, with plenty of time to contemplate their pasts and futures. In modern writings, a person is designated "dying" if a terminal illness, such as inoperable cancer, has been discovered. A long time may pass between this point and the patient's actual death; the person may be hospitalized and rehospitalized several times; the illness may appear to be in remission, and family members will gradually be told and decide who else to tell. To some extent the hospital environment itself determines the experiential nature of dying, since most staff are too busy to spend much time with terminal patients. A current alternative to hospitals, the hospice, is an institution designed explicitly for the terminally ill; its major goal is to provide for a comfortable and good dying. Given the emphasis in the current literature on acceptance as a goal, this seems a valid alternative. Traditional hospitals would sometimes enforce an ethic of "keep on fighting" and might condemn a patient for "giving up," even when there is no longer a realistic chance of recovery.

The first of the stages postulated by Kübler-Ross is called "denial" and covers a wide range of specific behaviors. Denial can mean the initial "I don't believe it!" when confronted with news that one's illness is terminal (this is an almost universal reaction). Often it extends to an absolute refusal to admit that one is very sick. A patient, while insisting that she is merely run down and expects to be going home any day, will also be aware that she is receiving radiation treatments daily. This is a situation frequently reported in today's literature. There is also a good chance that persistent deniers used this technique to ward off unpleasant realities when they were healthy. In this case, should a counselor try to effect drastic personality changes or let the patient remain as is until she wishes to talk about the illness? Another variation is the patient who knows perfectly well she is dying and will talk about it to someone—a nurse's aide, say—while denying to family, doctor, and interviewer.

The other stages, like denial, cover a range of behavior. Anger can be expressed in the urgent demand for ultimate justice (as characterized by Job), or by bickering with the hospital staff. Since anger is a normal reaction to frustration and helplessness, those surrounding the patients must realize this and understand the latter's predicament. Sometimes anger takes very irrational forms, such as when cancer patients blame their relatives for giving them the disease. Some persons have been angry their whole lives, and will continue to use anger and defiance as a generalized stance toward living, as in the case of Revolutionary War hero, Ethan Allen.

> His minister said to him in soothing tone, "General Allen, the angels are waiting for you." And Ethan Allen replied, "Waiting, are they? Waiting are they? Well, let them wait!"[6]

Because this kind of "heroic" defiance is culturally idealized, patients are often encouraged in this direction.

Bargaining refers to the secret pleading made by many patients: "If God lets me recover, I will devote myself to Him," or variations on this theme. Since most persons keep their bargains to themselves, it is difficult to obtain information on this stage.

Depression, or sadness (we prefer the less psychiatric term), is, along with denial, the universally reported finding associated with dying.[7] This is natural and understandable grief at the prospect of losing life, relationships, and possessions. The amount of grief experienced bears no relationship to the objective value of that which is being left behind; a mother of five small children may show and feel less grief than an elderly spinster worried about the fate of her cat. It seems that even in ages past, when belief in a positive afterlife was universal, persons about to die wept for the loss of life's goodness and blessings—not always, as we shall see, but often. A distinctively modern expression of sadness, however, is the lament over a wasted or meaningless life. Tolstoy's story, "The Death of Ivan Ilyich,"[8] expressed this magnificently several generations before modern "Thanatology" had come into being. Dying here is the occasion for despair over never having really lived—not for having lived a wicked life. This latter sentiment, and the accompanying fear of hell, is absent from all contemporary accounts. According to Kübler-Ross, persons who have been "ambitiously controlling" and interested in material goods and superficial friendships (like Tolstoy's hero) are those most likely to despair when confronted with impending death.[9]

When Kübler-Ross stated that the final stage, the goal of the process, was acceptance she did not mean joy or resignation but something in between.

> Acceptance should not be mistaken for a happy stage. It is almost void of feelings. It is as if the pain had gone, the struggle is over, and there comes a time for "the final resting before the long journey" as one patient phrased it.[10]

The dying person does not so much give up or abandon hope but rather gives in to a natural awareness that the end is near. Kübler-Ross compared this state with infancy, when "nothing was asked of us and all that we wanted was given."

> And so, maybe at the end of our days, when we have worked and given, enjoyed ourselves and suffered, we are going back to the stage that we started out with, and the circle of life is closed.[11]

Notice that this image of the closing circle potentially conflicts with the patient's own image of a long journey about to be started. But the purpose of Kübler-Ross' remarks about infancy and "the circle of life" is to uphold an attitude of willing surrender, rather than to insist on heroic defiance of death. It need not be an indignity or an affront to one's individuality to participate in a cycle of life shared by all living beings, whether or not there is another stage of a journey to come. When a ninety-year-old woman states that she is ready to die and be with God, most current psychological writers would feel that this constitutes "acceptance." The devaluation of this life implied in some afterlife belief systems can be a denial, but it can also be a realistic appraisal of the terminally ill person's sufferings and loss of zest for living. In this situation we see that, while dying as ending may dominate contemporary literature, the older model of dying as transition is still viable.

DIGNITY, AUTONOMY, AND RIGHTS

As we have seen by now, the self-help literature is dominated by an ideal of autonomy, self-determination, and a fear of being or remaining a victim. However implausible this ethic may be when set against the Kübler-Ross progression toward acceptance of the inevitable, it is resolutely maintained by many popular writers.

> We really have only one of two choices in regard to suffering and dying—either we attempt to find meaning and stay in reasonable control of our destiny as long as conscious intellect remains, or we allow ourselves to be caught up in futility and hopelessness and give ourselves over to someone else for control.[12]

Against this right to remain in control of our destiny are arrayed the power of institutions—doctors and hospitals— and also other powers that be.

> In all societies, the structure of power, of State or Church, has consistently rejected any idea likely to give the individual power of choice in matters of life or death, or freedom of action in accord with his own private conscience.[13]

It should be the individual's own right to determine when, how, and under what circumstances to "let go" and accept death. This letting go is turned from a passive to active experience, since it must or should be done in my own style, on my own terms, and on a timetable set by me. Popular writers do not doubt that a "good death" is the individual's own responsibility. "It is the patient's responsibility to arrive at a sense of when life is over in general and when he or she in particular is ready for a timely death."[14]

It seems appropriate to ask if this insistence on autonomy and self-control constitutes a higher-order denial by authors of books with titles like *Coming to Terms with Death.* Surely one aspect of coming to terms with death is encountering and acknowledging my own basic lack of choice in some matters, my own will's subordination not to church, state, or society, but to nature itself. In a society decisively committed to autonomy and active manipulation, this giving in appears as victimization. The extreme emphasis on choice, autonomy, and self-sufficiency in much popular literature may mask a great fear of any letting go. As one author triumphantly asserts: "I have chosen to be born and I will choose to die. What a relief. The burden of my being a victim, hunted by death, vanishes."[15] Here one can definitely talk of denial: it is not within the grasp of any human being to choose to be born, and our deaths are inevitable. We can embrace this situation, bemoan it, and hasten our own deaths, but to speak of choosing birth and death makes no sense in this context.

There is something skewed about a literature which insists that we face death honestly and openly, but at the same time upholds an autonomy ethic as ultimate. In many situations, of course, autonomy can and should be increased. For instance, many doctors worry about whether to tell a patient that illness is terminal. Yet, "If a person's life is really his, if it really belongs to him, then the first essential question is his right to the truth about himself."[16] As with sexuality, emphasizing autonomy and self-sufficiency in this context involves a reordering of priorities and a fresh appraisal of many traditional positions. This is particularly true when authors ask if the individual has a right to a quicker but more conscious death than might be possible with current life-prolonging techniques.

Is it better to let the patient help determine under what conditions various measures should be used? Popular writers often address this complicated issue as if it were a clearcut choice between autonomy versus submission to the power of institutional medicine, with an advocacy of "my right to die" perceived as preferable to dependence on medical authority. If it is true that it is "in self-control and the right to participate that dignity resides,"[17] then the preferred alternative will be whatever augments the voluntary, self-determining qualities of the patient. Little trust exists that others—namely doctors or family members—will provide genuine support or that their assistance will genuinely further the dying patient's own autonomy.

We find an overall equation in the self-help literature on dying of "dignity" with "self-control." Death with dignity became a slogan; what was meant was death with autonomy and a maximizing of the dying person's right to determine the circumstances of his/her own end. But is this the most accurate meaning of dignity, and if so, why are there no books titled *Sex with Dignity* or *Dreaming with Dignity,* since these are exactly the values espoused by inner-experience advocates on these topics? In an interesting account of the concept of dignity, ethicist Leon Kass proposed that this term has been somewhat misunderstood and misused by most contemporary writers. The central and original meaning of dignity, according to Kass, is "Worthiness, elevation, honor, nobility, height—in short of excellence. . . . Dignity is, in principle, aristocratic."[18]

Nothing could be further from the overall moral and religious intentions of self-help literature than such an aristocratic concept. In fact, honor and nobility go sharply against the extremely democratic stand of all inner experience literature, which maintains the frontier person's distrust of elites and authorities. Psychological writings are universal in appealing to generic human potentials and in minimizing "natural" differences among persons even when these exist. For instance, it is alleged that some women are naturally more orgasmic, or certain persons are spontaneous lucid dreamers, but such claims never help sell how-to-do-it books, designed to aid everyone to have such experiences. In contrast, "dignity of soul" is a quality which certain human beings possess, and is revealed in their actions, including their dying. According to Kass, it is not a universal right. Kass' own argument and his critique of the popular literature on this issue reveals contemporary psychology's deep American commitment to democracy, and its transformation of what began as an aristocratic ideal into a goal for all, and a right for which all should struggle.

This insight can be extended to explain a feature of inner experience religiousness which might be otherwise puzzling—its lack of named heroes and saints. Other religions have their founders and popular leaders. But psychological religiousness of the kind we are exploring does not venerate Freud, and in fact makes fun of the veneration Freud's followers have shown. Jesus and Buddha are great individual founders, but for Maslow the ideal was an individualistic piety in which each peaker became his/her own founder, and the need for models and heroes vanished. It is true that for some who are deeply involved in humanistic and transpersonal psychology, certain figures have functioned as gurus (Fritz Perls, R. D. Laing). But it is possible to be a devotee and enthusiastic exponent of psychological religiousness and inner experience without citing these figures by name, or being particularly knowledgeable about them as individuals. Kass's discussion of dignity suggests a correlation between strong repudiation of all belief in special aristocratic excellences and this loss of interest in venerating heroes and leaders. Anonymous designations such as "all the world's great mystics" or "peak-experiencers everywhere" replace particular great-souled personalities.

Kass himself suggested that pleas for death with dignity

were really demands for death with fewer indignities. This may, in itself, be a worthy goal and more realistic than an ethic of self-sufficiency in which one chooses both birth and death. An indignity is a specific circumstance that tends to inhibit the expression of dignity; current literature on dying certainly documents these indignities, which can and should be eliminated. But this is a far more modest goal than the individual's absolute right to self-determination, and does not necessarily involve the theme of self-control versus victimhood central to popular writers.

ON THE BRINK OF DEATH

For some eras past, the moments immediately prior to death were given intense religious significance. There would be some internal cue that one's time had come, after which attention was to be turned toward final preparations for ending this life in a state of grace and entering the next. Pain, doubt, and despair were the enemies at this time; the medical aspects of dying ceased to be interesting or relevant, since it was as eternal soul that the transition took place. A sudden death was a terrible evil, for it robbed the person of this chance to make proper preparations. Such an understanding of dying, which dominated Christianity for most of its history and which has direct parallels in other traditions, is universally perceived by contemporary writers as a thing of the past. It depended on a firmly held mythology of the afterlife, an explicit separation between soul and body, and the fundamental importance of the soul's relationship to God.

There were times when the traditional view of the near-death state was used to support a complete devaluation of this life's goods, or a sickly sweet portrait of a perfect afterlife. In an 1850 book, *Death-Bed Scenes,* compiled by Davis W. Clark, a Christian minister, these themes are paramount. A good believer was expected not merely to accept death and hope for the mercy of God at the Last Judgment, but to welcome dying enthusiastically, as a transition to eternal happiness. The following case history illustrates this attitude: a nineteen-year-old newly married woman who had hoped to be a missionary in India was dying. She refused to be cheered up with thoughts of recovery and told her doctor, "You ought rather to pray that I may depart, that I may be perfectly free from sin and be where God is." But her ideas of death centered on meeting mother and friends in heaven. She told her husband:

> Jesus will be your best friend, and our separation will be short. We shall soon, very soon, meet in a better world. If I thought we should not, it would be painful indeed to part with you.[19]

Overall, death appeared to her as glorious and she was eager for it. This attitude was used as a model of a good death by the compiler. In the section entitled "Dying Sinners" one finds accounts which would win the praise of contemporary secular authors for the acceptance and dignity they reveal, but they are condemned by the Evangelical compiler for their lack of joy and enthusiasm for the glorious afterlife.

These materials, from the *Ars Moriendi* literature of the Renaissance through the later works, give some perspective on twentieth-century understandings of dying. If one followed a model in which death was a glorious transition, then the entire psychology of dying might be very different from what one finds in studies of persons dying today. Yet today some authors are re-discovering the older, traditional views of the time just preceding death. Partially due to Kübler-Ross' own influence and partially to the new openness about investigating experiences of dying, a lot of publicity has been generated about the transcendent and out-of-the-body experiences which occur at the brink of death. Raymond Moody's *Life After Life*, its imitators, and now some more research oriented studies have opened up an inner experience which may have been commonly known to past ages but which had to be "rediscovered" in our time.

Out-of-the-body, near-death experiences provide classic examples of situations in which experiences were suddenly rediscovered, publicized, and advocated. The experience itself may be rare, but nowhere near as rare as most of us once supposed. Kübler-Ross, Moody, and others began collecting cases where individuals reported a separation of consciousness and body and/or an extreme state of bliss and peace at a moment when life was threatened. Other aspects of this phenomenon include a speeded-up review of one's whole past life and a journey through a "dark tunnel."[20] Soon other persons came forward with similar accounts, delighted to share an experience they had kept secret (sometimes for years). These experiences are clearly the memorable, "putting up a plaque" sort on which the inner-experience literature rests. They suggest to all who have had them (including nonbelievers in traditional religions) that there is a blissful after-death state, a higher reality to which dying opens the door. "Suggests" is too mild a word; many experiencers would claim, "I don't just believe in an afterlife; I've seen it!" Whatever else these experiences do, they pull individuals toward a kind of acceptance far more vital and joyful than Kübler-Ross' stage five, without being world denying, as in the nineteenth-century young woman's ideal. Transcendent experiencers today sometimes encounter (or report to encounter) dead relatives, just as the young woman had hoped to do. God, Jesus, or a Being of Light also appear to many; it is not clear if any of these modern experiencers receive visions of hell, or if they would come forward to talk about them if such were the case.

We have linked these spectacular out-of-the-body, near-death transitions to acceptance of death, but at another level they could represent a fresh form of denial. Although the experiencers themselves may reach a new and deeply felt awareness that death is not the end, we suspect the veracity of the publicity such accounts have received, given a society which on the whole still denies death. It would be nice if these accounts "proved" that there is no such thing as death, and that the human being is truly an immortal spirit, but they really cannot. It would be more logical, but much less comforting, to claim that those who experience after-death bliss in this life will indeed be assured of immortality, while for the majority who do not, death is instead the closing of a circle.

What the rediscovery of transcendent, near-death experiences does, however, is reveal the paucity of philosophical reflection and the narrowness of secular writings on death and dying. A book such as *Life After Life* reopens fundamental religious questions wherein dying is historically considered part of the human condition but which modern how-to-do-it books repressed or ignored. Grappling with immortality, reincarnation, the symbolism of a perilous journey for the soul is part of dying—a part more universal than the issue of autonomy vis-à-vis the medical staff, or the right to be told about one's illness. Since the exact types of experiences publicized by Moody do not conform to any one traditional religious pattern, we are not dealing with Christian versus psychological religiousness. The difference is between psychological thinking at its less speculative and more secular and an emerging, nontraditional yet explicitly religious awareness.

The shift in interest from the five stages model to the transcendent model suggests a progression in the inner experience literature's own dynamic. An hitherto repressed experience is rediscovered, first in the naturalistic and clinical context of modern hospitals. As more interest in the experience is generated, facets are revealed which expand beyond the confines of ordinary pragmatic concerns. Dying as transcendent experience fits well within the religious nature of private experiencing, and the

Jamesian dichotomy between first- and second hand religiousness. Within this framework, the inner self's freedom is affirmed, not by emphasizing autonomy in relation to social institutions or one's alleged choice of life or death, but through a much more ancient ideal of transcendence. At this point, inner experience literature joins more directly with what is now considered transpersonal psychology and spirituality, the exploration of transcendent possibilities in dialogue with traditional systems for guiding the soul. We have traced the emergence of a religious dimension at several points in contemporary psychological writings, yet to a large extent it has remained either implicit, unelaborated, or far removed from all traditional reference points. This does not make it any the less religious, we would argue, but it requires the development of a new framework to see religiousness in the making rather than fully formed.

_____8

Inner Experience
and Contemporary Life

The language of some inner experience advocates leads to hopes for revolutionary and dramatic changes in human existence. Critics warn of the final downfall of Western civilization amid orgies of self-worship. We contend, however, that the inner experience literature fits comfortably within the framework of contemporary social conditions. In this chapter, we will examine the writings on inner experience from such a perspective.

A CONTEXT FOR INNER EXPERIENCING

It is in today's society that the rediscovery of dreams has occurred and in today's society that claims for the priority of inner, private experience are made. All the accusations of repression and extroversion notwithstanding, we have some reason to challenge the assumption that Americans are hostile to inner experience. Perhaps the advocates of inner experience are really congruent with other American cultural trends. And perhaps their writings can be placed side by side with other ways of valuing private experience, in order to highlight hidden similarities (hidden, that is, to most psychological writers).

The first claim has emerged in Western traditional religion, in popular religious developments such as the Charismatic renewal in Catholicism and the "born-again" Evangelical movement. As more traditional types of religious phenomena, these lie outside the scope of our study, but the appeal of both depends partly on a rediscovery of inner experiences such as conversion and ecstatic states.[1] Both movements value experientialism over doctrinal assent and certainly publicize the various intense inner states their members joyfully report. These popular religious movements show certain other continuities with psychological inner experience advocacy, such as frequent use of healing and wholeness as metaphors for personal transformation. Other features of the Charismatic and Evangelical movements are, however, sharply at odds with the inner experience literature we have examined; for example, a strong emphasis on the family.

The second instance of attention to inner experience is more dubious as evidence of the phenomenon of turning inward. If some Americans read books on getting the most from dreams and some report being born again, almost all are exposed to messages about headache, sore throat, muscle tension, backache, stomachache, nausea, diarrhea, constipation, menstrual cramps, and insomnia. These experiences, though hardly dignified, are "inner" and private. The products marketed to relieve these ailments are by now an enormous industry. To avoid repetition, we will use the phrase "headaches etc." as the referent for all of these experiences. One objection to these commercial messages as a source of data on inner experience is that so many of them are explicitly social and interpersonal in their orientation. Headaches etc. keep you from enjoying life with others and may drive others away from you. Advertisements for aspirin and laxatives, seen in this light, may be reinforcing our fears of social rejection, and are hardly oriented toward inner realities. However, many of these messages do emphasize the sufferer's discomfort, the feeling of not being oneself. These are appeals that depend on some sensitivity to inner states—noticing them and taking them into account as factors affecting daily behavior patterns.

If we accept, even tentatively, advertising for relief of headaches etc. as one additional set of materials focusing on inner experiences, then the latter are no longer so exotic as many psychological advocates would have us believe, nor is our culture so bent on repressing them. Neither is Western religion so devoid of intense experiencing as most psychological writers intimate, although in all likelihood, Christian experiential movements grew out of a recognized need for intense, private experiencing on the part of many church persons unwilling to desert their traditional faiths. Why, then, did some advocates of inner experience prefer a totally new, psychological context for their aspirations, however overtly spiritual their psychology occasionally becomes? And what is the relation between attentiveness to headaches and attentiveness to dreams and mystical states? We cannot accept an easy divorce between people's extraordinary experiences and their ordinary lives. What social arrangements permit and encourage preoccupation with inner states in all three of the contexts (popular psychological writings, Charismatic renewal, headaches etc.) we have mentioned? Before we can adequately address this question, we must first clarify a matter which we have left vague up to this point—the meaning of the term "religion."

THE MEANING OF RELIGION

When nineteenth century pious writers talked of furthering the cause of true religion, they held clear notions of how to tell "true" from "false" forms of religion and what religion in any form looked like. So, as we have seen, do many of today's inner-experience writers. Although their criteria for "authentic" religion are certainly debatable, to ask, What is religion? in a scholarly context today is to ask a theoretical question which is genuinely open-ended. Religion in current scholarship is a certain type of human cultural activity, found in almost all societies and including a great diversity of specific expressions. Some traditional categories, such as idol-worship, play no role in the contemporary scholarly study of religions. Comparative religionists have found that nowhere are wood and stone and stars literally worshipped for themselves. These are considered among many peoples manifestations of sacred, transcendent, and invisible forces, "hierophanies" to use Eliade's term.[2] Since the beginning of the twentieth century, the scholarly study of religion, along with anthropology and other social sciences, has tried to develop conceptual frameworks adequate for what is now known about the immense range of activities, beliefs, and experiences which appear to fall appropriately under the heading "religion."

The nature of religion itself is no longer so obvious as it once seemed. What makes a nontheistic system, such as Buddhism, religious? Are the teachings of Confucius or Socrates religious as well? One choice has been to focus on a supposed core of all religion (as in Maslow's mysticism theory). For phenomenologists of religion, one school, religion is essentially defined by such terms as "the sacred," "the holy" or "the numinous"—conceived as a dimension of existence transcending normal empirical reality. But other researchers have found such a claim too amorphous to be helpful. Certainly, a conventional definition of a religious person as one who attends church regularly is unsatisfactory from many perspectives. (There are whole traditions with no permanent worshipping congregations, and there are many reasons why someone would attend church regularly other than religious devotion.)

Anthropologists in particular have been repeatedly confronted with churchless religions—societies where no special institution with a solely religious function exists. The religions of tribal peoples are sometimes very sophisticated but not easy to describe using categories drawn from Christianity. Psychological writers who object to "organized" religion would be pleased to know that in many societies there is no distinctively religious bureaucracy, but this does not mean that such societies are spontaneous, unstructured gatherings of individuals. They may be highly organized, but religion appears diffuse. Religion would be like an umbrella covering everything done among such peoples, rather than one institution alongside others. It is this feature which has led some anthropologists to offer more abstract, function oriented definitions of religion. Among these is Geertz's view of religion as:

> A system of symbols which acts to establish powerful, pervasive and long-lasting moods and motivations in men by formulating conceptions with such an aura of factuality that the moods and motivations seem uniquely realistic.[3]

This definition leaves many things open, but it allows for a wide range of beliefs, practices, myths, and moral teachings to be integrated under the heading "religion." Such a system of symbols, defined by what it does rather than its particular content, provides a model of the cosmos, and a model for human existence.[4] The "general order of existence" formulated by religion may or may not include a distinctively supernatural realm above that of this world. What is important is that some fundamental order is postulated, which can be appealed to in efforts to make suffering and other anomalies meaningful.[5] Such a definition treats religion as principally the activity of a society, or a group. Within that group, some individuals may be indifferent to an ultimate order of things, and others passionately concerned.

Is such an approach limited to the study of tribal societies? No, for it has already been applied to contemporary American religiousness as well. Does the American experience include a system of symbols which fills the same function as that described by Geertz? This system would not be identical to either Christianity or Judaism, although some of its components might be drawn from these traditions. Robert Bellah's landmark essay on "Civil Religion in America"[6] attempts to describe such symbols as found in American political life (particularly its most ceremonial aspects, such as inauguration speeches). Bellah traces a pattern of images which portray America as a nation in relation to some universal order of existence (not the literal worship of the American nation). Bellah, unlike many other writers who had read the same speeches, does not condemn this as idolatry because it differs from Christianity. Rather, he sees it as a form of religiousness running parallel to church religion, and having a validity of its own.

Another attempt to redefine religion more thoroughly along "functional" lines is Thomas Luckmann's *The Invisible Religion.*[7] For Luckmann as for Geertz, religion is a universal human activity. Although specific religious institutions have developed in the West, they are seen as the exception rather than the rule. Moreover, they are in the long run losing their hold over many sectors of modern life. Yet religion in the sense of a world view held by society continues; for Luckmann it makes no difference if the contents of the world view are God and salvation, or self and autonomy. Every society needs a world view (defined approximately as Geertz's "system of symbols") just as every society needs an economy or a political system, whatever institutions may or may not be present to serve any of these functions.

But Luckmann's theory may be extending the meaning of religion a bit too far. Anything existing in America probably shares in and helps express the "world view" of our society—even advertisements for headache remedies. We do not find it helpful to classify them as religious simply because they serve this function. It would be more accurate to say that because the world view of our society is expressed diffusely and through many institutions, no one institution or group has a monopoly on defining what the ultimate values or general order of existence shall be. Luckmann suggests that certain values and themes form the backbone of the modern world view, and these can be discovered both away from and inside churches ("invisible religion" is not always in direct competition with the visible kinds).

It is well to recognize that these definitions, which stretch religion well beyond traditional categories, arose in response to some of the problems also faced by inner experience writers. Many of the latter were openly and explicitly concerned with ultimate reality, the moods and motivations it engenders. Their writings fulfill all of the functions ascribed by Geertz to religion. Yet they were reluctant to label themselves religious for fear that this would be confused with churchly. Recalling Naranjo's poetic image of the root and seed of the tree whose branches are religion, we may discern a theme held by Luckmann and Geertz as well: the more hidden, fundamental processes which are religious are being brought to visibility. Whether they are recognized as religious by all, or even by those who hold them, they are becoming more and more potent. Thus Luckmann and Geertz suggest a way of defining religion which may help us grasp what "psychological religion" is about, how it functions.

But a few words of caution and explanation are in order. Any definition, in part, depends on the kind of inquiry at hand. Luckmann's theory is not useful for researchers engaged in detailed studies of church membership. Luckmann's view was meant as a critique of simplistic statements about secularization, but it is another matter to explain why certain groups of people join and attend churches when invisible religion is available to one and all. Moreover, neither Luckmann nor any other social scientist could legitimately claim that invisible, noninstitutionalized religion is better than the ordinary kind, although inner experience advocates are quick to judge the validity of anything by its distance from institutions. Nor does Geertz's definition help one in determining whether a religion is true. In his words, "an aura of factuality" must surround religious claims, and the portrait of the cosmos held by any religion must make sense and seem realistic. In order to be doing the work of a religion, a set of symbols must fulfill the function which Geertz described for a particular culture. However, to say that something is religious is not to say that it is necessarily a good thing, and certainly does not imply that it is true. For example, the symbol system of Hitler's Third Reich would undoubtedly be considered religious according to Geertz's definition, although the purpose for labelling it thus would never be to endorse the Nazi world view or justify its destructive consequences.

Such a definition of religion may strike many as abstract and too vague. Were we studying something which fit within traditional patterns, it would not be necessary to even raise the question of an overall definition of religion. But since Judeo-Christian categories have often been uncritically applied to phenomena outside that tradition with less than satisfactory results, it seems worthwhile to examine some of the attempts to overcome this traditional bias of method. Both Luckmann and Geertz also suggest, Luckmann very centrally, that no religion which really works will be disconnected from its social context. In fact, one might say that for both theorists, religion is a way of glimpsing that social context in its most profound dimension. This will help us orient our inquiry in this chapter. It will also invalidate some claims of inner experiencers to have discovered a religiousness completely liberated from any cultural conditioning or any social context.

MODERN SOCIETY: PUBLIC AND PRIVATE SPHERES

According to Luckmann, today's invisible religion can-not be understood without acknowledging a dominant feature of modern industrial society: the division between public and private spheres of life. The public sphere includes political and economic institutions, where functional rationality is the norm. Although the nation may exist "under God," no such ultimate sanction is offered for large corporations, and in practice public sphere institutions are functionally autonomous. The processes of large-scale industrial production breed norms of their own, such as maximalization (bigger is better) and the mental set which we have described as tinkering.[8] The public sphere has the unpleasant qualities of being too huge and complex for most persons to understand very well. Many of its workings are invisible and its international scope makes it even more remote from the average person. Of course, concrete manifestations of public sphere activities impinge directly on our lives; the rise in grocery prices reminds everyone how intricate and remote the workings of today's economy can be. The real cause of such happenings can be very hard to discover, and all stated causes (short supply, bad growing weather) are suspect. It is fair to say that over the last two decades mistrust in the public sphere and its representatives has increased massively[9] and there is no sign of its lessening.

The modern private sphere includes everything not part of the public sphere. The private sphere is not absolutely unregulated, but to a large degree each individual is given considerable freedom to select spouses, hobbies, careers, and ultimate values.[10] Voluntary associations, churches included, exist to help individuals pursue private goals. Some such associations are also important to the public sphere, or have a public sphere aspect to their existence (advertising, churches as owners of real estate). Others exist completely within the private sphere: a small group of friends meeting for prayer, consciousness raising, or dream sharing, for instance.

From a sociologist's perspective, there is nothing necessarily evil about the public sphere, or authentic about the private sphere. A religion which avoids being or looking like a large corporation is not seen as better than a religion with a large and visible institutional structure. Yet because it is within the private sphere that our own needs, rather than an institution's requirements take priority, it is clear how the private sphere is predominantly regarded as the locale for all that is authentically human and humane. The private sphere also lacks the mysteriousness of the public sphere. It is the realm in which one feels at home. It may be that one really does not know the private sphere any better than the public sphere, for the depths of the soul may remain as bewildering as the international currency exchange; nevertheless, one will feel more at ease with private sphere matters.

As Luckmann points out, these two spheres may be experienced as separate, although they are far more interconnected than most of us realize. The public sphere's boundaries determine the private sphere's scope. Generally, private sphere changes have little direct impact on the public realm[11] but may indirectly influence it in many ways. Norms generated within the public sphere, and firmly established there, have a way of insidiously creeping into private sphere matters. For example, the entire tinkering attitude, when applied to dreams or sexuality, represents such an invasion of the private sphere by a public sphere norm. The private sphere is simply too amorphous and unstable to generate an equally persuasive set of norms which everyone can accept.

In the modern private sphere, persons are left to their own devices to construct stable identities by selecting and incorporating bits and pieces from a huge assortment of possibilities. This has been likened to shopping in a supermarket and is appropriately termed "the consumer orientation" by Luckmann.[12] Traditional socialization, in contrast, meant adhering to an obligatory set of roles and the values that went with them. But today, even those who try to resist the hazards of consumer identity by choosing to be traditional illustrate the workings of the consumer orientation, since how traditional and in what ways are mostly a matter of private decision. There are, however, some real limits to this process. Persons from disadvantaged backgrounds are, in practice, excluded from much of the supermarket. Although identities constructed according to consumer principles are constantly being revised, rearranged, or traded in, restrictions endemic to humankind must be considered; it is not realistic for one to begin a career as a ballet dancer or a basketball player after a certain age. Often, those who wax enthusiastic about the consumer orientation tend to overlook these real limitations.

A sociological formulation locates the idea of hidden possibilities in a very unusual social context rather than a universal human nature. Consequently, the choices from which to pick—the contents of the supermarket—are stripped of potential transcendence. In light of Luckmann's consumer orientation framework, the meaning of "potential" in the inner experience writings becomes more concrete. If socialization is no longer acquiescence to imposed traditional role patterns, then the flexibility and endless possibility for change which modern identity formation produces means that an ideology stressing undiscovered potential and downplaying limitations will be plausible. For the inner experience advocate, potential connotes something detached from what one already is, and almost beyond imagining.

For Luckmann, the private sphere is all of a piece, and religion—as a world view or sense of ultimate values—is squarely within it.[13] Religious groups have many competitors all equally lodged within the private sphere: therapy groups, family camping, and almost any hobby or private pursuit can in fact perform some of the same functions as religion. Yet because of the traditional Western pattern of the permanent local congregation, it seems more cautious to restrict religion to the model of religious groups or communities. To many, the new religious consciousness meant the presence of new religious groups in America, groups with belief systems, permanent members, and institutional arrangements. But under today's private sphere conditions, there is no reason to assume that religiousness requires membership in a permanent group—at least no sociological reason.

Psychotherapy, which is a highly successful private sphere activity, has never been ordered into local permanent congregations. Clients come together to meet with the therapist (in group work) but presumably have no permanent investment there. Most therapy groups, training groups, and encounter groups disband when their task is accomplished or after a certain predetermined number of sessions. Members may remain on a mailing list, or may have contact with the therapist from time to time, but presumably no longer have a continuous need for therapy. The transient nature of such psychological groups is even more apparent in those workshops and weekends which are open to the general public. Here one can talk about customers, who disappear back into an anonymous mass after the event is over. There are of course some conspicuous consumers who return again and again, but this is different from permanent membership in anything. Although for therapy to succeed a warm interpersonal climate must exist, officially, psychological groups are contractual and depend on a professional selling specific services to customers.

In our view, the inner experience literature represents a definite stage on the way toward deemphasizing group membership altogether. Inner experience advocates occasionally recommend getting together with a friend, and some of the authors run workshops. But group activities are so clearly an end to a private, individualized goal that, should they prove unsatisfactory or unnecessary, the preference would be to drop them and work by and with oneself. There are all sorts of dangers to groups, especially groups which have a definite stake in their own long-term survival. Also, the expense of psychological workshops or therapy is no small factor; one major selling point of self-help is that it costs very little.

Surely this casual and transient approach to group membership fits the consumer orientation well. Commitments may be made for a limited period of time, or on a tentative basis. No permanent bond is created between the individual and any specific organization. The degree of involvement, and its duration, is left flexible. If we want to talk about psychological religiousness, then, we should not expect to find a "psychological church" or any equivalent body. And if we take Luckmann's theory seriously, we will see why this is unlikely to be a popular option: current identity formation is too fluid a process to be aided by irrevocable or permanent commitments, which are seen as possible burdens. Although this outlook on commitments has had a devastating effect on marriage, family life, and Christian and Jewish congregations with many file-card members, it is hardly an issue for a religiousness where membership is beside the point.

PRIVATIZATION

We have already suggested that certain popular conceptions found in the inner experience literature derive their plausibility from the structure of the modern social world. The consumer orientation encourages a belief in unlimited possibilities and perpetual change—also, alas, perpetual discontent with what one already is or has. We have also noted the very strong tendency (all but built into the system) to turn the private sphere into the "authentic" realm, letting the public sphere sink into irrelevancy or generalized mistrust. One might speak here of the "repression" of the public sphere, but we hesitate to draw on such a psychologically loaded term to describe this neglect.

A privatized world, one in which "ultimate values" and identity are separated from participation in major institutions, not only means that groups will be mistrusted, or viewed as existing essentially for individualized ends. It also means that the really massive power of the public sphere factors will be minimized or overlooked entirely, a problem to which Luckmann and others[14] have called attention. For amidst all of the demands that inner experiences be taken seriously, and claims that inner experiences can revolutionize our lives, remarkably little attention is given to the ways our society might actually help publicize and promote such experiences. Because of their intense preoccupation with individual self-sufficiency, psychological writers do not explore how television, for instance, might be used to expand our appreciation of dreams, as it has already been used to help expand our sensitivity to headaches etc. Other major industries and modern organizations could leave room for and encourage inner experiencing in a variety of contexts, without requiring any revolutionary changes in their basic functioning.

Let's take a few examples of these possibilities. In Philadelphia, a local TV station began broadcasting sports fantasies. Viewers wrote in to tell their favorite sports fantasies, and the announcer arranged to have some of these come true through enactment on camera. Like Nancy Friday's *My Secret Garden,* this was a way to tell viewers that it's OK to fantasize—however silly the fantasies, they are fun. Similarly, imagine a televised dream sharing group, where the dream is presented visually, then discussed with group members (viewers could phone in with questions and suggested interpretations). Inner experiences could also be promoted by airlines; the mystical potential of above-the-clouds flight is real enough, and might be publicized as a way to get the most out of flying. By stressing the extraordinariness of flight, passengers would have the chance to transcend their usual preoccupations and participate in a new awareness of nature's immensity. Airlines could offer brief training classes for passengers made anxious by this possibility (as some already do for persons who are frightened to board a plane for any reason). These examples are neither far-fetched nor impossible to implement. "National Daydream Day" or a special holiday to honor the courage of dying persons are a little more implausible.

Why are there no such suggestions as these in the inner experience literature? Is it because they are impractical or utopian? No. In fact, they take for granted and take seriously the powerful entrenchment of advertising and media in our society. We believe that this is the precise reason why no inner experience writers seem the slightest bit interested in making such suggestions. Advocates of inner experience do not wish to remind readers of mass communications and other realities which bring to mind the public sphere. They prefer these to remain "invisible" while the private benefits of dreams, etc. are being extolled. Besides, much of the criticism leveled at modern society implies that, were private experiencing honored as it should be, all the fragmentation and alienation of today's world could be overcome. Suggestions which show a world which both honors inner experience and retains all the basic institutions and frameworks of the current world are unwelcome. Airline companies, television shows, advertising: all of these could remain as they are while explicitly endorsing inner experiences. This may also be the reason why current American sensitivity to the internal body sensations of headaches etc. is unmentioned by authors who locate our civilization's problems in its lack of attention to inner states.

It seems that whatever changes inner experiences may produce, basically their chance to restructure the public sphere is extremely remote. Thus their effects on our everyday modern existence will be limited in scope. The public sphere's power, unknowability, and remoteness generates discomfort and a sense of helplessness which how-to-do-it authors take for granted and seek, with little success, to overcome. Perhaps how-to-do-it authors can patch up and rehabilitate victims, but they cannot prevent victimization or the pervasive sense of adriftness which the consumer orientation can bring. They foster what Luckmann describes as "an illusory sense of autonomy"[15] generated by the nature of the private sphere and the invisibility of the public realm.

The privatization process goes beyond the repression of public sphere realities. In Luckmann's theory, the private sphere is all of a piece, a warm and friendly realm particularly when contrasted with the public sphere. But in the inner-experience literature, it is not all of a piece—some portions of it are more authentic than others. Remembering the notion of concentric circles as a model for the self, we may say that in this literature, the private sphere may stand for the various levels of a journey—from public to private. For instance:

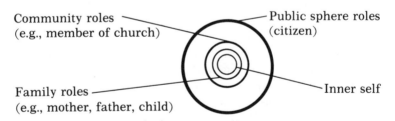

Community roles (e.g., member of church)
Public sphere roles (citizen)
Family roles (e.g., mother, father, child)
Inner self

For many inner-experience writers, only the core of the circle is fully trustworthy. All the outer layers are contaminated, perhaps by their association with public sphere institutional realities. Even family roles, as perceived in much psychological literature, are dehumanizing and have an anonymous, imposed aura to them. To say that we are the sum total of the roles we assume is anathema when extreme privatization lets the outer circles stand, but withdraws ultimate significance from them. Taxpayer or scout leader are not where one's true identity lies, and in fact one's true self is incompatible with any public, social expression or formation. An intensely privatized ethos thus suggests no new, authentic roles to play, but either condemns all "role-playing" or advocates mistrust of it.[16]

One of the spokespersons for inner experiencing responded to charges of privatizing by declaring "We are already privatized; we are becoming interiorized."[17] She was correct insofar as the inner experience writers did not create the private sphere; they found it already existing and are trying to get the most from it by pushing its privacy to the limits. The consumer orientation aids these efforts, by giving all external, social components of identity a tentative, transient, and fragmented quality. The consumer orientation, like the advertising which relies upon heightened sensitivity to minor discomforts, feeds on and creates yearnings, dissatisfactions, and wistful imaginings on a vast scale. It augments a sense of footlooseness and a constant feeling of victimization by forces far outside the individual's control. In response to this, the inner experience literature seems to ask, "Given the world as we know it, how can each individual get things to work for him or her?" Therefore, it is easy to criticize its approach as selfish and simplistic, furthering the kinds of attitudes which ignore the underlying social conditions which created many of the problems.

THE AUTONOMY ETHIC

The favorite values of inner-experience writers are: autonomy, self-sufficiency, self-control, self-acceptance, and the intrinsic benefits of experiencing for its own sake. These values have been condemned as narcissistic by critics.[18] Narcissism is an exaggerated, immature belief in the self as the center of reality. Narcissistic people are incapable of forming any deep and lasting relationships with others; they find themselves infinitely alluring. There is the additional implication that the narcissist's "self-love" is the opposite of the genuine self-acceptance which characterizes the mature loving personality; the narcissist's passion is a cover-up for a basically unsatisfactory and loveless relation to the world.

The accusation against inner experience literature is that it promotes just this kind of preoccupation with I-me, that those values which stress relatedness with others and a moral obligation toward them are neglected. To make the depths of the self so central, enticing, and authoritative is to go against an ethic which values justice and charity over self-fulfillment. The rhetoric of self-sufficiency is criticized as a shrill denial of the real situation.

> Our lives are crowded with the presence of unacknowledged others upon whom our well-being and privilege depend. The shadows of those neglected others—dying in Asia, hungry in Africa, impoverished in our own country, fall upon every one of our private acts, darken the household and marriage bed for each of us. We try to turn away, but even the desperate nature of our turning is a function of their unacknowledged presence. . . . Something in each of us . . . aches with their presence, aches for the world, for why else would we be in so much pain?[19]

Although there are narcissistic persons in every movement and all over the world, inner-experience detractors state that this ethic of selfishness and gloating over the self is occurring at a time when Americans' moral obligations to the rest of the world are becoming more imperative than ever.

It does seem that the inner experience writers are guilty

of this at many points. Sexuality, a mutual situation, is reinterpreted so that the I-me experience of orgasm becomes its goal. The ideal of personal fulfillment is not loving service to others or love for and with others, but to fly high, not having to pay the price, and not to be a victim. Mystical religiousness has neither systematic theological content nor a system of ethics; "B-values" such as Goodness, Beauty, etc. do not show one how to live justly, truthfully, and compassionately. In hundreds of places throughout the literature, the self and its hidden depths were valued above all else, and the self's human responsibilities to others entirely ignored.

But some of the literature seemed a bit more subtle. Is the true self which is the source of wonder and enthusiasm in our literature the same as the narcissist's self? Some writers make a distinction between Self and ego, and many are clear that the true self is not identical with one's in-the-world, day-to-day personality. It is just this personality which is seen as unsatisfactory and in need of expansion, transformation, and transcendent grounding. When it is stated that fundamentally we are universal, impersonal energies—All That Is—and not individual souls with name tags attached to them, one can legitimately question whether Self here bears any resemblance to the ordinary meaning of the term. Perhaps this issue parallels that of the Judeo-Christian misunderstanding of "idol worship" mentioned earlier in this chapter. It is not the empirical self which is being worshipped, but the transcendent reality manifested in the self. Unfortunately, this line of argument falls down when it is clear that the self meant by many popular authors is not a cosmic transcendent reality such as one finds in the classical Hinduism of the Upanishads (where the Atman, or cosmic self, is said to be identical with the ultimate reality of Brahman). Instead, the self of the psychologists is merely the empirical personality writ large, so to speak, and given central attention. The literature on sexuality and dying clearly addresses the ego, and stresses competence, rationality, and autonomy. Nor does capitalizing the *S* in *Self* necessarily move Western readers away from an identification of ego and toward the more cosmic conception. The self as a hierophany, a source of sacred and numinous power, is one of the themes we will examine in the next chapter.

The consumer orientation does give to the individual self (in the ordinary sense) an incredible burden of responsibility. Luckmann's entire discussion is based on the premise that in all premodern societies socialization meant appropriating a few traditional roles and trying to live these out with honor and dignity. The modern individual is burdened with the task of constructing an identity, a process which places a premium on qualities such as flexibility, initiative, and respect for others' rights to their own choices. The implication is that in some fashion the individual self is as important in this context as in that of inner experience writers. The rationale offered for stressing the importance of the self may vary from "God grants the soul immortality" to the language of hidden infinite potential. But if the consumer orientation works roughly as Luckmann suggests it does, then these rationales are not wish-fulfillment and narcissism, but disguised acknowledgments that contemporary identity formation is to an unprecedented degree, an individual task.

It is not our intention to claim that the virtues associated with the consumer orientation are better than those of traditional societies. We, in effect, are all stuck with the consumer orientation whether we explicitly accept its values or not. Where psychological writers seem to have an advantage over those from more traditional perspectives is that the former have learned to accept the pluralism and diversity which is part of the contemporary social world. Psychological religiousness accommodates itself to a diversity of life-styles and goals, admittedly often by stripping these of moral dimensions (we recall the image of hollandaise on the asparagus). While for most Western religion pluralism poses a threat, the psychologically oriented inner experience writers are much more inclined to welcome it as an opportunity, strongly condemning any attempts to coerce others into compliance with their own value systems or life-styles.

There is another point to consider. Many popular psychological works are clearly aimed at persons unsure of themselves and their capacities. Such persons, burdened with a sense of their own inadequacies, are less than likely to have been engaged in meaningful social or communal activities prior to encountering the writings of popular psychology. If it were the case that they had busied themselves by feeding the poor, comforting the sick, visiting the imprisoned, and fighting for racial justice until, upon reading *My Secret Garden,* they dropped all former pursuits and enthusiastically cultivated sexual fantasy, one could clearly blame inner experience literature for providing an "awareness trap."[20] However, there is no indication that anything like this is the case. One might well argue that only a person with some self-confidence and sense of responsibility for himself can be considered capable of genuinely aiding others, or cooperating in the long-term and very difficult effort to change social structures. Luckmann, writing as a sociologist, points out that most students of contemporary society have been more intent on evaluating it than understanding it.[21] The split between public and private and the consumer orientation need to be understood before they are condemned as "dehumanizing" or their effects over glamorized as in much of the rhetoric on hidden human "potential." Moreover, there may be good political and ecological reasons why the kind of social order we know, and the religiousness it engenders, may not survive very long, thus raising a set of problems for which no one has certain answers. But given this social order, psychological religiousness has some advantages and a great deal of plausibility. In the final chapter we shall turn directly to its theology, its principle religious ideas.

Psychological Religiousness

Our task in this chapter will be to state some principle theological themes of psychological religiousness. The focus will be on both its occasional continuity with and its radical departures from traditional forms of Western religions. Many of the motifs implicit in the analysis of particular inner experiences will become explicit here, for psychological religiousness is our category, designed to draw forth the assorted claims about ultimate reality found throughout the inner experience literature. It is now time to present these claims as a coherent system, and subject them to serious scrutiny.

THE QUEST FOR AUTHENTIC RELIGIOUSNESS

At the outset, we may ask if psychological religiousness is indeed best seen as an alternative to ordinary forms of Christianity or Judaism. If so, then for many persons the quest for spiritual fulfillment is undertaken explicitly through psychologies emphasizing inner experience. The well-publicized activities of the Human Potential Movement have attracted such persons. For other individuals, an interest in inner experience might supplement a more formal and public commitment to a traditional religion. The ethos and ethics of much of the inner experience literature would have to be discounted, refuted, or carefully evaluated if persons in this situation were to maintain any consistency in their belief systems and norms for behavior. A third possibility is that the world view of psychological religiousness can, in actuality, infiltrate the traditional believer's understanding of his or her faith. Here, the content of Christianity will be translated into the language of popular psychology and gradually be absorbed by the latter.

How might this occur? Christianity and Judaism are both struggling to represent their traditional contents in ways that will have immediate relevance and plausibility. Almost forty years ago, Rudolph Bultmann addressed this problem, with his call to "de-mythologize" the Gospel by translating its original content into the language of Heidegger's existentialism.[1] Surely the language of popular psychology, far more accessible than Heidegger's, could also be a candidate for a fresh presentation of the central Christian message. The inner experience writings could then be seen as a vehicle for making Christian faith contemporary and relevant. The explicit hostility of many of the psychologists to traditional forms of religiousness would have to be glossed over, or dismissed as a product of ignorance.

In our view, a major obstacle to this project is the deep incompatibility between the major religious themes already present in the inner experience literature, and the basic contents of traditional Western faiths. By bringing to light the aspects of psychological religiousness discovered in these writings, we hope to demonstrate that popular psychology is not religiously neutral, and that its own indigenous spirituality should not be ignored. One effect of such a presentation should be to increase scepticism and caution about the use of popular psychology in such a Bultmannian translation project. Another effect, we hope, will be an attempt at a serious evaluation of psychological religiousness as a spiritual alternative in its own right, an alternative already preferred by many persons.

Since most inner experience writers see themselves as offering alternatives to Western traditions, does the very presence of psychological religiousness represent the failure of Western religions to speak to people today? Most psychological advocates of inner experience would agree to such a view, and there is certainly a great deal of evidence to support them. A recent study shows mainline churches unable to hold a heavy proportion of their nominal members;[2] it is more than likely that this group forms the bulk of the readership for how-to-do-it writings and other secular self-help works. Persons affiliated with fundamentalist or other very conservative churches (which seem to have stronger holding power) might be less open to psychological religiousness, or perhaps feel less need for it.

There is, however, an ironic twist to this reading of the story. Psychological religiousness sees itself as a partial replacement for the moribund religions of the West. But in many ways it shows more continuity with American popular piety than with either Freud or with "scientific" psychology. Perhaps what inner experience religiousness represents, even more than the failure of Western religious traditions, is the failure of psychology as a science to answer religious questions. We would characterize the work of the popular writers, by and large, as "folk science." Although some begin by sounding scientific, they frequently evolve into rhapsodic communication over Being, body-energies, and Ultimate Reality. The repeated claim that "Only you are the expert" is another way these writings divorce themselves from any ordinary criteria of scientific verification. Standard Western ideals of science, it seems, have failed these inner experience advocates as badly if not worse than Western religions.

What we claim is that as a religious alternative, psychologists' faith in inner experience has plausibility and coherence. Because it emerges directly from modern living conditions it does not require demythologizing effort. It speaks clearly to many modern persons, offering hope for vital and renewing connection with what it sees as the real powers of the universe. Without duplicating all the functions of traditional religion, it endeavors to help us reach the roots of our being. At its best, it holds out the hope that modern persons can experience life as good and beautiful and joyous, and helps them overcome conditions which prevent the full realization of such a vision. We believe its exact claims should be examined and taken seriously. Even if the result is not profound, complex, or sophisticated religion, it may well have something important to offer.

Much of the inner experience literature is concerned very explicitly with "authentic" religion. As these advocates have defined it, religion is an individual inner apprehension of the ultimate nature of reality, a mystical experience which can never be expressed adequately in words. As such, anything else that calls itself religion is the product of human social conditioning, which all too often has served to stunt human growth and discourage many persons from any involvement with religion at all. Such an understanding is shared by almost all of the inner experience advocates. By contrast, theoreticians such as Geertz and Luckmann do not equate real religion with intense private experience, but consider religion an activity of an entire society.

The inner experience advocates have inherited from their Judeo-Christian background an insistence on separating true religion from all other forms. Our own perspective, however, will deliberately avoid this path. We will not assume, along with Maslow and so many others, that private mystical experience comes closer to the core of religion than, say, communal worship. But we will eschew criteria about authentic and idolatrous faith drawn from Christianity or Judaism. Idolatry is an enormous preoccupation for the Jew or Christian who sees in some psychological writings the deification of the self.[3] (There are, however, other traditions where the concept of "idolatry" is not found. Even psychological religiousness avoids the term "idolatrous" when referring to what it sees as repressive, conventional forms of religion.)

Other writers have assumed a standard of doctrinal or psychological authenticity against which they measure various forms of faith. This leads to certain sorts of generalizations which we shall do our best not to repeat. For instance, we shall avoid statements such as "Psychologists are optimistic about the self's potentials," or "Christians believe that man is essentially sinful and unable to save himself." Many advocates of both psychology and Christianity enjoy such statements, since each side can assume the other is clearly in error. Unfortunately, judgments of optimism and pessimism about the self are hardly helpful; it is not clear whether the self being argued over is the same creature, or what the grounds for optimism really are. Christians have been optimistic about the final destiny of the soul, the resurrection of the body, and the life in the world to come. For many believers, these hopes have far outweighed any emphasis on original sin. And one may discern without too much difficulty a solid core of pessimism in many inner experience writings concerning both human relationships and the salvation of modern society. (In contrast, both liberal and neoorthodox Christianity appear wildly optimistic on this issue.)

A variant of this ideal of authentic religion involves linking contemporary psychological religiousness with ancient movements, particularly Gnosticism. C. G. Jung was chiefly responsible for popularizing such a link and glamorizing Gnosticism. For critics, "neo-Gnostic" becomes a synonym for "heretical"—i.e., wrong religious-ness. Jung's view was that Gnosticism was superior to or-thodox Christianity;[4] he saw his own psychotherapy as very close to Gnostic religiousness. We are sceptical of drawing such parallels, even without the negative conno-tation of Gnostic as heretical. Psychological religiousness is a product of contemporary social conditions, which are not those of the ancient world. Moreover, while there may be some pockets of modern spirituality which continue the Gnostic preoccupation with a spiritual elite, a small and secret gathering of those in the know about salvation, nothing could be further from the outlook of most how-to-do-it authors. Their intent is to democratize and publicize, as we saw especially in the discussion of their reinterpre-tation of the meaning of dignity. For our purposes then, psychological religiousness is not primarily a rediscovery of religion's true, eternal core or a new edition of an an-cient heresy. It is a modern form of faith, serving as an alternative to traditional concepts of faith and existing within the context of the consumer orientation and the private sphere.

ANTITRADITIONAL RELIGION

The idea of a new religion seems intrinsically difficult for humankind. What appears to be a new religion to non-believers is for insiders a rediscovery of ancient teachings, or a contemporary revival of an ancient faith. Very few of the new religions of the sixties and seventies were really brand-new, and all but a few saw themselves as continua-tions of some ancient tradition. The alternative route taken by other groups was to disclaim religion-hood en-tirely (for example, the Science of Creative Intelligence). It seems that religion is naturally associated with the idea of a tradition. The key idea for us behind the notion of tradition is that of a set of symbols or values received from a previous generation and handed down to the next. Or at least this is the intention of those within the tradition, to whom generation can mean one's own biological off-spring, or spiritual children such as disciples. The ideal of tradition takes seriously precisely those linguistic and cultural forms, learned through socialization, which inner experience advocates consider unnecessary and oppressive.

In psychological religiousness, the link between true religion and tradition disintegrates. Psychological religiousness, which does not form a church, does not wish to become a tradition either. Some wish to inaugurate an era founded on each experiencer's own private religion.[5] Although there are hundreds of how-to-do-it books on child-raising and parenting, the literature we have examined is for adults seeking to free themselves of cultural programming received from their parents, not for parents and prospective parents concerned over what religious instruction to give their children. Indeed, the average reader addressed by the inner experience advocates is neither child nor parent, but that anonymous, autonomous, somewhat footloose participant in the private sphere's world of consumer orientation. Such a person does not feel a part of any continuing tradition, or even a continuing family structure. Intensely aware that much of what was taught by parents (who believed in handing down beliefs) proved dysfunctional, unbelievable, or otherwise inadequate, such a reader will be wary of trying to impose personal convictions on offspring. Certainly, psychological advice-givers insist that such wariness is proper. Throughout the inner experience literature, family life is discussed in overwhelmingly negative tones, as a process of brain-washing from which individuals need liberation. From this perspective, a desire to hand down one's religiousness to one's children would be considered symptomatic of a repressive outlook. Here, the inner experience advocates seem unable to provide any positive vision of mutual responsibility and communication between generations.

Behind the rejection of the "tradition" model lies the pervasive disgust with language we have already noted, and for which humanistic therapy movements have often been criticized. It is no twentieth-century discovery that certain religious experiences cannot be adequately captured by ordinary language. But in the past, solutions to the problem of communicating such experiences included the development of special linguistic forms, doctrines of analogy, or of mystical silence. When psychological religiousness rests itself on ineffable experiences, it draws a very different conclusion: words don't count. If ultimate reality lies beyond language, in a realm outside of all cultural conditioning, then any language is misleading and basically worthless. Words represent the culturally shaped realm from which one needs to escape. As a result, there is a positive contempt for language at many places in the inner experience literature. For example,

> Sorry, dear reader, but you also are a bit too much in your head. Otherwise, you wouldn't be reading these yakety-yakety words of mine. You'd be out digging in your garden or playing tennis or making love.[6]

For many inner experience advocates, all language is just so much "yakety-yakety."

Few traditional mystics reached such a conclusion. These persons were often careful about which phrases they used to approach an experience impossible to describe. They were concerned lest the ignorant misconstrue their expressions, or take phrases literally which were meant spiritually. Although some mystical writers may have used language carelessly, it was not their deliberate intention to do so. In contrast, given the striking contempt for mere words shown by psychological writers, they show little motivation to choose just the right phrase, or to clarify exactly what they are claiming. The overall attitude toward one who would ask for such precision in language would probably be impatience or the suggestion that the enquirer should do some gardening or lovemaking instead of worrying about such head matters.

Alas, one must make some use of words in order to write a book which communicates ideas. And since the core of the inner experience literature is firsthand accounts of what it was like to have the experience, it is impossible for the authors of this literature to discount language totally. Yet the belief is widespread that language distorts and hides reality rather than reveals it. "If culture programs us through words, direct experience transcends words."[7]

This view could be described as a naïvely optimistic appropriation of the Sapir-Whorf hypothesis, which held that language does indeed structure and determine our reality by programing us to see the world in a certain way. The psychological writers' appropriation of this idea is naïve, for when taken seriously, the Sapir-Whorf view suggests that it is all but impossible to escape cultural conditioning and certainly much more difficult than inner experience writers claim. In fact, their entire view of the relation of man to language may be in error, as it depends on an image of humanity finding some island safe from the sea of language and from this vantage point looking over the world. At least some philosophers have explicitly denied that any such dry land outside the world of language could be a genuine human possibility.[8]

What are the religious consequences of the psychologists' disgust with language and their hope for a realm without words? Such an attitude is a striking rejection of one of the basic symbols of Western faiths. In the West, the Word and God's creative speech have always been prominent theological themes. As one theologian put it, "God's love for the world can only be imparted in words,"[9] and the image of God in man has been traditionally associated with the human capacity for speech and reason. Western religion has not seen words as obstacles to God, but as intrinsic to revelation. Therefore, which words were used became, at certain times, a terribly significant question; words had a power to them and in them; they counted. Thus creeds and ritual formulas were not mere yakety-yakety, interfering with some higher nonverbal apprehension of the divine. Words were used in praise of God by men and angels, and for many persons the belief that God spoke became concretized into a faith that written Scriptures contained His exact words.

One consequence of rejecting both tradition and language is an indifference to and ignorance of the past as a vital element, infusing meaning into the present. For inner experience writers, our own culture's past provides neither role models nor figures of wisdom for us today. The exotic past of ancient mystics and primitive shamans flourishes, but such figures are interesting principally because of their discontinuity with today's individuals. As critics have pointed out, only the present, the here and now, really exists for some inner experience advocates.

> If we do not have to look beyond the present, any record-keeping or symbolization of language would be unnecessary. Language is useful only for recurring situations, and to refer to things absent in the present situation.[10]

The loss of the past is the other side of an extreme emphasis on immediate experience, for the past, by definition, will be second hand. To a person firmly committed to such a stance, verbal religion—catechisms, creeds, liturgies, even the words of the Bible—will probably be just so much yakety-yakety, and never a living heritage.

THE DIVINE AS FORCE

For readers of this work who saw the movie *Star Wars,* the idea of one cosmic, beneficent "Force" to which individuals can connect themselves and from which they can draw power will sound rather familiar. But it must have taken a certain amount of preparation to make such a conception plausible to Westerners (I have never found anyone yet who simply did not understand the idea of such a Force, although no one I know took the movie's belief system literally). One source of such preparation has surely been contemporary psychology. In the inner experience writings, universal and helpful forces—sometimes named with capital letters—are a constant presence. The individual reader is given advice and instruction for making contact with such forces and on how to benefit from them. Without equating inner experience religiousness, which is meant to be taken fairly seriously, with *Star Wars* (which was meant as entertainment), we may say that they emerged from the same contemporary matrix, which Luckmann termed the "world view."

The exact names of the impersonal forces discussed by inner experience advocates vary: the unconscious, being-values, body-energies, dream-power. Or the author may just refer to "nature," or "the universe" and mean by this a totality which utterly transcends ordinary apprehension. The popular writers who spoke of "Being, God, All That Is, and the Universal Mind"[11] may have been closer to the truth; basically, it doesn't matter what term is used, since all words are inadequate anyway. The qualities ascribed to this many-named force are: ultimacy, activity in the sense of creative energy, power, awe, mystery, beneficence, transcendence of the ordinary ego, universality, ineffability, and peace. The force is natural—in opposition to all cultural fabrications—and yet it has much of the transcendence traditionally ascribed to supernatural reality in the West. This force promises us a way which will bring peace and happiness and a sense of power not based on aggressive domination of others or repression of self. One can say of it:

Long life is in her right hand;
  in her left are riches and honor.
Her ways are ways of pleasantness,
  and all her paths are peace.
She is a tree of life to those who
  lay hold of her;
Those who hold her fast are
  called happy.   (Proverbs 3:16–18)

Of course, ancient writers personified. Just as God was "He," Wisdom was "She." This is exactly what contemporary psychological writers, with few exceptions, will not do. Whatever energies lie within, waiting for us to contact them (or striving to get our attention) they are not fundamentally persons but powers. Even the original Jungian emphasis on the personifying nature of archetypes has given way—in American writings which make use of Jung's thought—to an overall focus on energies and forces which pervade awareness or into which one is absorbed. These images are the norm; language of encounter with an Other, a Person who addresses me, is absent. One schizophrenic autobiographer used the image of waves on a dry beach; the idea of an Ocean of Being is also found in the more Maslowian writings. Even Dream-Power, to which one can pray, is hardly a person—perhaps as Wisdom for the ancient writers was not a goddess, but a deliberately personified principle created by God.

For some psychologists, impersonal language is used because it sounds less mythological. For others, it sounds Eastern, although the average knowledge of Eastern religions among these inner experience advocates is minimal. For a few, language of forces and energies sounds more scientific. As should be apparent by now, popular psychologists are sufficiently alienated from their scientific heritage not to press this argument very hard. A few do suggest that modern physics also postulates universal energies. The world as portrayed by the physicist may be the world apprehended by the mystic[12]; both have abandoned ordinary language as inadequate for the task of communicating such a reality. This idea, which has a very definite appeal to the theoretically inclined and/or the scientifically trained, makes only a sporadic appearance in the popular inner experience literature. When readers are searching for ways to get the most from their dreams, they presumably do not want to be regaled with lengthy expositions of quantum theory or relativity. Hence, it may be sufficient that talk of energy sounds scientific, although the actual context is spiritual-mystical.

But psychological religiousness avoids describing the ultimate in traditional Father-Son terminology, and the notion of God as a Person is relegated to the context of childhood religious beliefs (which readers have presumably outgrown). In works which are preoccupied with the self, with persons and their problems, the notion of a divine Person who loves us, or wants us to be all that we could be, never appears. Some psychologists would say that any belief in such a Person is a childish fantasy, but few popular writers can afford to make this kind of direct statement. It would offend readers, and besides, how-to-do-it writers are themselves rather too vulnerable to the criticism of purveying childish fantasies. We may discern in this avoidance of family metaphors for God not only an extension of the aforementioned hostility to family life, but the real inheritance of Freud. It was Freud who cast doubt on all unselfconscious analogies between earthly and heavenly fathers by showing how complex and ambivalent the attitudes of children toward their parents may actually be. The consensus seems to be that Freud spoiled Western religion for sophisticated persons—one of the few points at which Freudian views are assumed rather than discarded. (Many theologians would violently disagree with this, of course, and might point out that Freud interpreted the oceanic experience of the mystic as the return to infancy!)

However, the overwhelming preference for impersonal force language to describe ultimate powers at work in the self and the cosmos has still another source. The modern person's experience of power is by and large anonymous; the powers-that-be are the institutions of the public sphere, not named identifiable individuals such as kings. In America today, gigantic impersonal forces are often perceived as running things; for example, big business, the liberal establishment, the military-industrial complex, or simply bureaucracy. In the private sphere, powerful persons (i.e., one's parents) however impressive, are perceived as relatively insignificant when compared to the public sphere powers. Perhaps, given the hiddenness and mysteriousness of the public sphere, a form of religiousness not bound to traditional images will incorporate the experiences of immensely powerful forces into its portrait of the cosmos. What is of course not borrowed from perceptions of the public sphere is the sense of mistrust which most people feel toward whatever runs things "out there." Dream-Power, the Unconscious, and Being are all posited as trustworthy and good as well as powerful, which evidences the minor role scientific language actually plays in psychological religiousness. Scientists may talk of energy fields, but they do not maintain that energy fields are good or beneficial in any moral sense. By contrast, inner experience advocates universally uphold the ultimate goodness of the powers they have discovered at work in the cosmos. Perhaps only such impersonal and beneficent ultimate forces can outweigh the everyday experiences of the huge but untrustworthy public sphere.

But if these forces are good, in the sense that Being itself is good, then what of evil? Is there a dark side to Dream-Power, Being, the Unconscious, as there was a dark side to the Force in *Star Wars*? The answer is rather difficult to discover from the inner experience literature. Insofar as our limited apprehension of ultimacy makes us vulnerable to fears, distortions, and projections, there are certainly negative experiences in store for many of those who come into contact with the inner, ultimate powers (this, we may recall, was a major theme of those who wrote on madness). But, for psychological writers, evil beings have no existence as realities in themselves; the monistic mysticism they proclaim prohibits such a possibility. The non-peakers were not cosmic-level demons, or even irrevocably evil persons, but rigid, overly rational, and basically frightened individuals. For Maslow, "the dangers of Being-cognition" are real, but derive from human ignorance, fear, and limitation. For Jungian authors, a key to self-knowledge is confrontation with "the Shadow," the dark side of oneself. However, in the interest of having readers pursue the path to self-knowledge, most writers either minimize dangers, or stress that with basic trust in the forces at work, one can overcome the negative, painful aspects of experience, or learn to deal with these creatively. What no inner experience writers allow for is the possibility that an extremely evil person might discover these same forces and use them for his own selfish and destructive ends, as in the stereotype from folklore and fairy tales of the evil magician, of whom the *Star Wars* villain was a contemporary representative. But there are real, living persons who do come close to embodying this cultural archetype (Charles Manson is perhaps the most likely candidate). A good reason why psychologists do not bother to discuss such a possibility is that their helpless, "victimized" readers do not need to be warned against power and control, but seem desperately in need of strength and self-confidence. We may also speculate that the fascination with occult powers, evidenced by some of the inner experience writers, is a sign that readers can appropriate for themselves (in a very watered-down fashion) some of the magical asocial powers traditionally associated with sorcerers.

We wonder whether the idea of an ultimate, impersonal, and beneficent force utterly negates traditional Jewish-

Christian ideas about God. Some of these traditional ideas have been reinterpreted already within the most sophisticated theological contexts. Christian theologian Paul Tillich's conception of God as "the Ground of Being" beyond all God-symbols and personifications was so appealing to Maslow[13] that it probably helped him formulate his view of peak-experience religiousness. Current interest in the Holy Spirit as a healing power is dramatically on the rise among Christians. The Holy Spirit is the least personified aspect of God in the West, and lends itself to language of power, force, and energy (as when the Holy Spirit's healing power is described as flowing "like electricity" through one's body). It is not absolutely clear to this writer that the language used by the psychologically religious could not be incorporated into Western religion, but taken by itself, psychological religiousness significantly departs from traditional emphases on God as Father, and Jesus as Son; on images of Lord, King, Savior, Shepherd, Judge, etc. All of these expressions point toward personal power or caring, and inner experience religion ignores them entirely.

THE SELF AS HIEROPHANY

The concept of the self in inner experience writings has received more negative attention than the other religious ideas held by the advocates. The fondness of some writers for capitalizing Self or True Self adds fuel to the fires, since in English, capitalization of such words is usually taken to indicate Deity. It is beyond our power to determine exactly how seriously most inner experience advocates do mean to deify the self. It seems that in the actual context of their writings, this question is left obscure, deliberately ambiguous. The ego, the ordinary personality, is consistently described as helpless, bewildered, cut off from basic forces which could guide and renew it. But to what extent is the True Self, the point within which such renewal occurs, a divine being? The term hierophany, from Mircea Eliade's writings, means "a manifestation of the Sacred."[14] We maintain that the True Self functions as such a manifestation for inner experience religiousness. It is not itself literally divine.

As we have seen, "God" in psychological religiousness is a term linked casually to the impersonal Forces we have just described. These manifest themselves through the core of the self. But the Unconscious, Dream-Power, etc. are never literally worshipped, and most writers use the term God as a synonym for Ultimate Reality, but loosely— they wish to imply something vast and vague. Thus we are really not describing pantheism as a theological doctrine, in the sense that Christian tradition has known theology, or that philosophers such as Spinoza or Emerson were pantheists. What can I do to plug into my True Self? is the recurring motif of inner experience advocates; questions about the exact metaphysical nature of the True Self, its divine status or ontological basis, are not. Curiously, what might be philosophically vague often has a symbolic power to it which carries weight, for evocative rhapsodic language is, for many religious people, closer to the truth than the language of systematic theology. Not all vague language about God is rhapsodic (some can be just ill-formulated philosophical discourse!) but psychologists seem to hold that the Forces they have discovered, and the Self where these Forces are manifest, invite praise and awe rather than exact objective description.

Given these factors, we can suggest the following generalizations about the religious status of the self in this literature. None of these should be taken as applying uniformly to all of the inner experience materials.

1. The innermost core of the person is where sacrality and truth can be found, if they are to be found anywhere. For inner experience advocates, the Kingdom of God is within you—so exclusively *within* that what distinguishes our literature is the extreme pessimism it

shows over finding anything authentic outside the experiencer's own inner being.

2. The True Self exists in potential, as an unlimited set of possibilities. At the same time, it already is: it is discovered and not yet to be created. Unlike the Sartrian existentialist, the inner experiencer does believe in an internal essence. This may be expressed as a universal human nature, or a True Self hidden underneath the social roles. This belief in a primordial core self acts as a counterforce to the tinkering mentality. It also may help provide individuals adrift in the modern world with the same security obtained by the traditional Christian who trusts in God as the unchanging eternal Rock. At some point, then, the Self is prior to all efforts of manipulation on our part, or acts of will.

3. The Self's unlimited potentials include much that is supernatural or at any rate superordinary. These superordinary powers, contrasted with the paucity of our daily lives, reveal the immense otherness of the true powers and forces lying within. Lucid dreaming, out-of-the-body experiences, and mystical sex all point us toward such otherness, a realm of pure freedom. Like the Kingdom of God, however, this realm now exists only in a hidden, elusive way. The lonely mystic, the mad person, the person in the throes of orgasm or dying, can make contact with it. But its powers are not yet manifest on a large scale in today's world, or even in much smaller scale interpersonal contexts.

4. "Not yet" is, for most of today's inner experience writers, a future state of society, one in which inner experiences are taken seriously and the West turns inward to overcome its materialism and alienation. In the most explicitly Messianic image, advocates spoke of "Putting the first man on earth,"[15] and this certainly captures the spirit of fervent hopefulness which dominates some of these writings. Yet there is little inclination to be more specific about the new age to come, especially about its social and institutional forms.

Although some writers see a focus on the self as Eastern, there is little serious attempt to incorporate traditional Eastern spiritual motifs such as renunciation and disciplined detatchment. More typically, contemporary American pursuit of orgasm is equated with the Buddhist experience of the Void, or the liberated sexual morality of *My Secret Garden,* and is looked upon with the nonjudgmental attitude of the Zen master! From these examples, one can fairly say that no serious appropriation of any Eastern tradition has occurred, although there are psychologists now interested in such an integration. In popular psychological religiousness, "Eastern" functions as a convenient symbolic alternative to Western rationalism and repressiveness. Rarely are Eastern perspectives introduced to critique the psychologists' own spiritual claims.

Ironically, psychology has, for a long time, been accused of atheism, materialism, and holding a mechanistic and rigidly secularist portrait of human nature. The majority of inner experience advocates, determined to correct these impressions, have tried to develop a view of the person which leaves a large space for spirituality and religious experience. This they have done, only to be bitterly criticized for deifying the self or promoting pseudoreligion. We clearly do not find the latter charges fair. Inner experience advocates have a religious consciousness of their own which differs from what traditional Christianity and Judaism continue to uphold. Because the psychologists' religiousness does look to the self and gives intense spiritual centrality to forces manifest only in the self, it is easy to mistake their claim for a view which turns the empirical ego into a divinity. At least to some extent, psychological religiousness tries to ensure a separation between our ordinary selves and that hidden core of Self which is at bottom identical with a universal, impersonal Force permeating the cosmos. Such a Force forms the basis for matter and consciousness, and symbolizes the totality of All That Is. Perhaps this is egotism writ large, but if so, then the same might be said of the traditional

Western ideal of an eternal soul with a name recorded forever in God's Book of Life.

IS PSYCHOLOGICAL RELIGIOUSNESS ADEQUATE?

The ideas we have just summarized constitute the core of inner experience advocates' religious claims. Given their extreme individualism, one ought not to expect any interest in ritual, communal worship or the collective and institutional side of religion. They have simply extended, to its logical extreme, the Jamesian and Protestant bias against all externalized ritualistic religiousness, and endorsed an interiorized, individualized form of faith. The Self as hierophany in an alienating world, and the Self's continuity with impersonal beneficent universal forces: these are the themes of psychological religiousness, and on them it bases its promise of individual liberation and wholeness through harmony with the cosmos.

How does one evaluate the truth or falsity of such a religious claim? Of what value are the testimonies and case histories found in the literature itself? Christians and Jews can measure the claims of psychological religiousness against their own standards of theological orthodoxy, and cite testimonies from their own traditions. But for the religiously uncommitted, such standards or accounts may have little relevance. For the scholar of religion, judgments about the claims of a particular religion are notoriously difficult to formulate. Social scientists such as Geertz and Luckmann deliberately avoid this issue entirely. It is almost inevitable that when judgments are made, they will reflect the theological commitments of the theorist. For example, Mircea Eliade views all religion as manifesting the Sacred, and, therefore, as in some sense true. But in his writings, his actual criteria for an adequate manifestation of the Sacred depend on a highly idealized view of archaic-primitive "natural religiousness."[16] Modern phenomena are suspected as counterfeits or degenerations. We do not find this attitude helpful in evaluating the inner experience advocates and their religiousness.

For exponents of psychological religiousness, the inner self or Self is trustworthy. The source of evil is located externally, at the periphery of the person, and in all visible social roles and institutions. Between the Self as hierophany and All That Is, no disjunction or discontinuity can really exist. We have already indicated, in the last chapter, that this may engender a callous moral stance toward the real responsibilities and interdependencies which we, as affluent Americans, may share with others around the globe. An "I-me" orientation will not help prepare us for accepting fuel shortages, or a future of shrinking economic possibilities. Yet, without seeming callous ourselves, we wish to bracket this very serious moral concern, and focus our attention and our evaluation on the portrait of the inner Self depicted in psychological writings. It is here that psychological religiousness focuses its attention, and it is here that its outlook seems most plausible.

Let us also, for the present discussion, eliminate the crasser and more obviously hedonistic examples of psychologists' visions from our evaluation. While we found many indications that "to fly high, not to have to pay the price!" was an ideal for inner experience advocates, we also found a great many qualifications and repudiations of that goal. Awe, mystery, and gratitude for the power of dreams, the Unconscious, and the True Self were not absent from our literature. With this in mind, what are some of the strong points, the places where we find psychological religiousness offering some adequate alternative spiritual answers? There are three which we can emphasize:

1. To be able to identify with and trust one's own experiences is a prerequisite for any adequate appropriation of religiousness at a personal level. In an era of pluralism, and a consumer-orientation process of socialization, the inner experience literature holds forth a reli-

gious ethic which makes direct experiencing a necessity, and a genuine possibility for all. Even given the
problems of separating direct experience from cultural
programming, we would say that any religiousness
which hopes to retain the loyalty and inner assent of its
believers must follow this pathway.

2. The language of energy fields, nature, and All That Is
can act as a corrective to a manipulative and domineer-
ing posture toward nature and one's body. Although
such language is, at times, trite and sentimental it provides an implicit counterweight to the extensive reliance on technology and tinkering so often found in
today's literature. Psychological religiousness offers a
vision of nonexploitative harmony and fulfillment, for
those who can no longer conceive of the universe as
nurtured by personal forces such as the traditional loving Father of Christianity.

3. The universalism of psychological religiousness—its
attempt to focus on a transcultural core of mystical-
monistic experience—involves an acceptance of one
very important feature of the contemporary world. Our
world is one, and this requires a new understanding of
the truth-claims made by particular religious traditions. Those psychologists who attempt to express the
oneness of mankind by postulating a "natural" and non-
relative center within the self, and a universal religious
experience, actually follow a path laid out by the Enlightenment in its quest for natural religion. The results
show a certain similarity as well: an overall optimism,
and a lack of interest in religion as communal enter-
prise. For most inner experience writers, the claims of
particular historical religions pose a challenge and an
opportunity to discover the root beneath the tree, the
core which still contains life. Even if their specific formulations of this core are very much open to criticism,
it seems that in their refusal to avoid the problem of
religious relativism, they might encourage those still

within traditional faiths to rethink their own answers to this problem. The result may not yield one, worldwide religion, but it could prevent a retreat into a narrow, dogmatic absolutism.

These three features of psychological religiousness are countered by certain deficiencies and omissions which we find extremely serious. With the exception of the autobiographies of the ex-mad persons, nowhere in the inner experience literature do we find any real witness to those wells of melancholy in the self and the world which defy our best tinkering efforts. Nowhere is the enormous and well-attested capacity for self-deception really given its due. To mention this does not negate the importance of trusting one's own inner experiencing. In fact, we could argue that with an increased reliance on one's own inner resources, one is far more likely to discover one's capacity for self-deception. In the inner experience writings, on the contrary, no attention is given to this relationship. As a consequence, even the depths of the True Self, as portrayed in the inner experience literature, often seem shallow and banal. A sense of discontinuity, of being and remaining a problem to oneself—none of this finds expression in psychological religiousness.

To develop this criticism further, we can compare the religiousness of popular psychology with the symbols found in the world's major religious systems. In many of the latter, there are very central symbols for what theologian Paul Tillich called the power of "nonbeing,"[17] for suffering, separation, and moral brokenness. The theme of exile in Judaism, the Buddhist doctrine of *samsara* (the totality of the world conceived as suffering) and the Cross in Christianity all convey this. The role of such symbols is not to teach us that the world is a bad place and human existence meaningless. Their power lies in their ability to proclaim the presence of God or ultimate liberation even in those places and situations where all is lost or in despair. In such conditions, the underlying structure of all reality is perceived as suffering, as estrangement from God, as under the dominion of death. The divine appears fully enmeshed in the fundamental discontinuity and pain of all things. These images are not the final word for those traditions which hold them, but they are also inescapably present. No condition of eventual blessedness or liberation denies their power and reality. These are symbols of near-ultimate negativity, not merely in the social world but in our inner selves and in the very structure of the universe.

Psychological religiousness has no such symbols, no way to adequately express the paradox which these convey, a paradox of defeat–victory, bondage–freedom, death–life. Even if such themes might exist elsewhere in twentieth-century psychology, such as in Jung's work on the Shadow archetype, psychological writers on inner experience such as those we surveyed did not incorporate or develop such ideas. Certainly, the monistic mysticism adopted by most of the psychological writers omitted all reference to this kind of symbolism, or to the "dark night of the soul" reported by many traditional mystics. Perhaps most American have never been very adept at focusing on these realities, but psychological religiousness certainly continues an avoidance of themes of suffering and separation conceived as intrinsic components of existence.

But are suffering and separation, or the well of melancholy within the self, really intrinsic to our existence as human beings? Or are they thorns which can be weeded out of the garden of the Self? Perhaps by assuming that a religious system ought to consider suffering a central and nonaccidental matter, we are reintroducing in a covert fashion theological criteria drawn from traditional religions, in order to judge and condemn psychological religiousness. Our response to this criticism is that the traditional religions themselves grew out of an apprehension of the extent to which our lives as human beings are lived enmeshed in suffering. The specific symbols and doctrines they use to express this apprehension vary, but we would view their insight as both more profound and more adequate to the totality of lived experience than that of the psychological writers. Thus, the vision of psychological religiousness falls short of providing a fully adequate alternative to traditional religion for those modern persons seeking one.

Will its symbols evolve further, and deepen until they too can offer a vision of sufficient depth and complexity to overcome this deficiency? Will psychological religiousness continue as it has begun, flourishing among the religiously alienated and offering an optimistic and present-centered interiorized vision which coincides nicely with affluent social conditions? If social conditions change dramatically, will psychological religiousness fade away and be viewed by the next generation as a curious folk religion no longer the least bit relevant to their spiritual needs? We leave these questions for the reader and the future to answer.

Notes

CHAPTER ONE

1. William James, *The Varieties of Religious Experience* (New York: Collier Books, 1968), p. 24.
2. Ibid., pp. 24–25.
3. Martin Shepard, *Beyond Sex Therapy: A Manual for Discovering Personal Pleasure and Liberation* (New York: Penthouse Press, 1975), p. 14.
4. Jack Dowling and Robert Marmorstein, *Dreams and Nightmares* (New York: Harper and Row, 1973), p. 11.
5. June V. Regush and Nicholas M. Regush, *Dream Worlds: The Complete Guide to Dreams and Dreaming* (New York: New American Library, 1977), p. 154.
6. Shepard, *Beyond Sex Therapy* (inside cover).
7. Martha Crampton, "The Use of Mental Imagery in Psychosynthesis." (New York: Psychosynthesis Research Foundation, 1970), p. 11.
8. Georgia Kline-Graber and Benjamin Graber, *Woman's Orgasm: a Guide to Sexual Satisfaction* (Indianapolis: Bobbs-Merrill, 1975), p. 71.
9. Hans-Georg Gadamer, *Truth and Method* (New York: Seabury Press, 1975). This book contains the argument mentioned on page 11, particularly in Second Part, II, pp. 235–45.
10. James, *Religious Experience,* Lectures 9 and 10. See also William C. McLoughlin (ed.) *The American Evangelicals, 1800–1900* (New York: Harper and Row, 1968).
11. James, *Religious Experience,* p. 170.

12. Barbara Seaman, *Free and Female* (Greenwich, Conn.: Fawcett, 1972), pp. 212–13.

CHAPTER TWO

1. Peter Berger and Thomas Luckmann, *The Social Construction of Reality: a Treatise in the Sociology of Knowledge* (Garden City, N.Y.: Anchor Books, 1967), p. 98.
2. Havelock Ellis, *The World of Dreams* (Boston: Houghton Mifflin, 1925), p. 281.
3. Joseph Katz, *Dreams Are Your Truest Friends* (New York: Pocket Books, 1976).
4. Elsie Sechrist, *Dreams, Your Magic Mirror* (New York: Warner Paperback Library, 1974).
5. Ann Faraday, *The Dream Game* (New York: Harper and Row, 1974), p. 275
6. Carl G. Jung, "On the Nature of Dreams," in *The Structure and Dynamics of the Psyche, C.W.* 8 (Princeton: Princeton University Press, 1972).
7. Faraday, *Dream Game,* p. 12.
8. Ibid., p. 34.
9. June V. Regush and Nicholas Regush, *Dream Worlds: The Complete Guide to Dreams and Dreaming* (New York: New American Library, 1977) p. 111.
10. Tony Crisp, *Do You Dream?* (New York: E.P. Dutton, 1972), p. 45.
11. Herman H. Riffel, *A Living, Loving Way* (Minneapolis: Bethany Fellowship, 1973), p. 62.
12. Faraday, *Dream Game,* p. 142.
13. Crisp, *Do You Dream?,* p. 97.
14. Riffel, *Loving Way,* p. 67.
15. Regush and Regush, *Dream Worlds,* pp. 2–3.
16. Calvin S. Hall and Vernon J. Nordby, *The Individual and His Dreams* (New York: New American Library, 1972), p. 104.
17. Patricia Garfield, *Creative Dreaming* (New York: Ballantine Books, 1976), p. 94.
18. Regush and Regush, *Dream Worlds,* p. 7.
19. Katz, *Your Truest Friends,* p. 16.
20. James J. Donahue, *Dream Reality* (Oakland, Cal.: Bench Press, 1974), p. 51.
21. Garfield, *Creative Dreaming,* p. 14.
22. Regush and Regush, *Dream Worlds,* p. 5.
23. Kilton Stewart, "Dream Theory in Malaya" in *Altered*

States of Consciousness, edited by Charles T. Tart (Garden City, N.Y.: Anchor Books, 1972), pp. 161–70. This essay, whatever the accuracy of its data, is the source for contemporary psychologists' interest in the Senoi.

24. Garfield, *Creative Dreaming,* p. 111.
25. Regush and Regush, *Dream Worlds,* p. 156.
26. Katz, *Your Truest Friends,* p. 98.
27. Charlotte Beradt, *The Third Reich of Dreams* (Chicago: Quadrangle Books, 1966), p. 21.

CHAPTER THREE

1. Mary Watkins, *Waking Dreams* (New York: Harper and Row, 1976), p. 18.
2. John Calvin, *Institutes of the Christian Religion,* edited by John T. McNeill (Philadelphia: Westminster Press, 1960), I, v, 12.
3. Max Weber, *The Protestant Ethic and the Spirit of Capitalism* (New York: Scribners, 1958).
4. Henry A. Murray, "Techniques for a Systematic Investigation of Fantasy," *The Journal of Psychology* 3 (1936): 115–43.
5. Eric Klinger, *The Structure and Functions of Fantasy* (New York: Wiley Interscience, 1971), p. 10.
6. Ibid., p. 181.
7. Ibid., p. 222.
8. Jerome Singer, *Daydreaming: An Introduction to the Experimental Study of Inner Experience* (New York: Random House, 1966), pp. 66ff.
9. Ibid., p. 76.
10. Ibid., p. 58.
11. James Thurber, "The Secret Life of Walter Mitty," in *The Thurber Carnival* (New York: Harper and Row, 1975).
12. Singer, *Daydreaming,* p. 27.
13. Martha Crampton, "The Use of Mental Imagery in Psychosynthesis" (New York: Psychosynthesis Research Foundation, 1970), p. 3.
14. Nancy Friday, *My Secret Garden: Women's Sexual Fantasies* (New York: Pocket Books, 1974), p. 8.
15. Ibid., p. 33.
16. Ibid., p. 10.
17. Ibid., p. 6.
18. Carl G. Jung, *Psychology and Alchemy, C.W.* 12 (Princeton, N.J.: Princeton University Press, 1970), pp. 203–4.
19. Ibid., p. 204.

20. Author's spontaneous fantasy.
21. James Hillman, *Re-Visioning Psychology* (New York: Harper and Row, 1975), p. 10ff.
22. Ibid., p. 39.
23. Ibid., p. 39.

CHAPTER FOUR

1. June Regush and Nicolas Regush, *Dream Worlds* (New York: New American Library, 1977), p. 156.
2. Abraham Maslow, *Religions, Values, and Peak-Experiences* (New York: Viking Press, 1970), p. 28.
3. Anonymous, appeared in *Fort Wayne Alternative School Newsletter,* no date (but published approximately 1973).
4. C. S. Lewis, *That Hideous Strength* (New York: Macmillan, 1965), p. 319.
5. See Lawrence LeShan, *The Medium, the Mystic, and the Physicist* (New York: Ballantine Books, 1975).
6. W. I. Stace, *Mysticism and Philosophy* (Philadelphia: J.B. Lippincott, 1960), p. 86.
7. Walter N. Pahnke and William Richards, "Implications of LSD and Experimental Mysticism," in *Altered States of Consciousness,* edited by Charles Tart (Garden City, N.Y.: Anchor Books, 1972).
8. Quoted in I. M. Lewis, *Ecstatic Religion* (Baltimore: Penguin Books, 1971), p. 37.
9. Arthur J. Deikman, "Deautomatization and the Mystic Experience" in Tart, *Altered States,* p. 36.
10. Ibid., p. 41.
11. Stanislav Grof, *Realms of the Human Unconscious* (New York: Viking Press), 1975.
12. Maslow, *Peak-Experiences,* p. 95.
13. Ibid., pp. 22ff.
14. Ibid., p. 72.
15. Ibid., p. 28.
16. Claudio Naranjo, *The One Quest* (New York: Ballantine Books, 1972), p. 10.
17. John Lilly, *The Center of the Cyclone* (New York: Bantam Books, 1973), pp. 158ff.
18. Stace, *Mysticism,* p. 47.
19. James H. Leuba, *The Psychology of Religious Mysticism* (London: Routledge and Kegan Paul, 1972; first published 1925), p. 309.

20. Wayne Proudfoot and Phillip Shaver, "Attribution Theory and the Psychology of Religion" *Journal for the Scientific Study of Religion* 14 (Dec. 1975): 324.

21. Gershom Scholem, *On the Kabbalah and Its Symbolism* (New York: Schocken Books, 1969), p. 9.

CHAPTER FIVE

1. R. D. Laing, *The Politics of Experience* (New York: Ballantine Books, 1967), p. 137.

2. Janet Gotkin and Paul Gotkin, *Too Much Anger, Too Many Tears: A Personal Triumph Over Psychiatry* (New York: Quadrangle, 1975), p. 383.

3. Lara Jefferson, *These Are My Sisters* (Garden City, N.Y.: Anchor Press, 1974), p. 199.

4. Mary Barnes and Joe Berke, *Two Accounts of a Journey through Madness* (New York: Ballantine Books, 1973), p. 273.

5. Quoted in Otto Friedrich, *Going Crazy: An Inquiry into Madness in Our Time* (New York: Simon and Schuster, 1976), p. 31.

6. D. L. Rosenham, "On Being Sane in Insane Places," *Science* 179 (Jan. 19, 1973): 257.

7. Mark Vonnegut, "Preface-Schizophrenia," in *The Eden Express* (New York: Bantam Books, 1976).

8. Laing, *Politics of Experience* pp. 128–29.

9. Gotkin, *Too Much Anger,* p. 4.

10. John Neary, *Whom the Gods Destroy* (New York: Atheneum, 1975).

11. Hannah Green, *I Never Promised You a Rose Garden* (New York: New American Library, 1964), p. 48.

12. Thomas Hennell, *The Witnesses* (New Hyde Park, N.Y.: University Books, 1967), p. 91.

13. Barnes and Berke, *Journey through Madness,* p. 3.

14. Ibid., p. 104.

15. Ibid., p. 148.

16. Green, *Rose Garden,* p. 208.

17. Gotkin, *Too Much Anger,* p. 354.

18. Barbara O'Brien, *Operators and Things: The Inner Life of a Schizophrenic* (New York: New American Library, 1976), pp. 97–129.

19. Kary K. Wolfe and Gary K. Wolfe, "Metaphors of Madness: Popular Psychological Narratives," *Journal of Popular Culture* 10:4 (Spring 1976).

20. Gotkin, *Too Much Anger,* p. 354.

21. Quoted in Laing, *Politics of Experience,* pp. 154–55.

22. Anton Boisen, *Out of the Depths* (New York: Harper, 1960), p. 91.

23. Gotkin, *Too Much Anger,* p. 377.

24. Laing, *Politics of Experience,* p. 133.

25. John Weir Perry, *The Roots of Renewal in Myth and Madness* (San Francisco: Jossey-Bass, 1976).

26. Roberto Assagioli, *Psychosynthesis* (New York: Viking, 1971), pp. 43ff.

27. Vonnegut, *Eden Express,* p. 98.

28. Ibid., p. 105.

29. Julian Silverman, "Shamans and Acute Schizophrenia," *American Anthropologist* 69 (1967).

CHAPTER SIX

1. William H. Masters and Virginia E. Johnson, *The Pleasure Bond* (New York: Bantam Books, 1976), p. 90.

2. Joy Warren, *How to Be an Erotic Woman* (New York: Award Books, 1971), p. 138.

3. Marabel Morgan, *The Total Woman* (New York: Pocket Books, 1975), p. 128.

4. Shere Hite, *The Hite Report: A Nationwide Study of Female Sexuality* (New York: Dell Books, 1976), p. 203.

5. William H. Masters and Virginia E. Johnson, *Human Sexual Response* (Boston: Little, Brown and Co., 1966.)

6. Masters and Johnson, *The Pleasure Bond,* p. 27.

7. Barbara Seaman, *Free and Female* (Greenwich, Conn.: Fawcett Publications, 1972), p. 13.

8. See for example, Georgia Kline-Graber and Benjamin Graber, *Woman's Orgasm: A Guide to Sexual Satisfaction* (Indianapolis: Bobbs-Merrill, 1975), pp. 4ff.

9. Hite, *Hite Report,* p. 82.

10. Ibid., p. 150.

11. Ibid., p. 151.

12. Ibid, p. 150.

13. Seaman, *Free and Female,* p. 145.

14. Seymour Fisher, *Understanding the Female Orgasm* (New York: Bantam Books, 1973), pp. 106, 219.

15. Kline-Graber and Graber, *Woman's Orgasm,* p. 71.

16. Hite, *Hite Report,* pp. 257ff.

17. Kline-Graber and Graber, *Woman's Orgasm,* p. 94.

18. Betty Dodson, *Liberating Masturbation: A Meditation on Self-Love* (New York: Bodysex Designs, 1974), pp. 26–27.
19. Masters and Johnson, *The Pleasure Bond,* p. 146.
20. Fisher, *Female Orgasm,* pp. 49, 192ff.
21. Seaman, *Free and Female,* p. 121.
22. Ibid., pp. 212–13.
23. Ingrid Bengis, *Combat in the Erogenous Zone* (New York: Alfred A. Knopf, 1972), p. 195.
24. Alex Comfort, *The Joy of Sex: A Gourmet Guide to Love Making* (New York: Crown Publishers, 1972), p. 51.

CHAPTER SEVEN

1. Stanislav Grof and Joan Halifax, *The Human Encounter with Death* (New York: E. P. Dutton, 1977).
2. Elisabeth Kübler-Ross, *On Death and Dying* (New York: Macmillan, 1969), p. 5f.
3. Philippe Ariès, *Western Attitudes Toward Death* (Baltimore: Johns Hopkins University Press, 1974), p. 14.
4. John Langone, *Vital Signs: The Way We Die in America* (Boston: Little, Brown and Co., 1974), pp. 331–32.
5. Kübler-Ross, *On Death and Dying,* chapters 3–7.
6. Cited in Marjorie C. McCoy, *To Die with Style* (Nashville: Abingdon Press, 1974), p. 59.
7. Richard Schulz and David Aderman, "Clinical Research and the Stages of Dying," *Omega* (Summer 1974) 5:137–44.
8. Leo Tolstoy *The Death of Ivan Ilyich and Other Stories* (New York: New American Library, 1960).
9. Kübler-Ross, *On Death and Dying,* p. 265.
10. Ibid., p. 113.
11. Ibid., p. 120.
12. Melvin J. Krant, *Dying and Dignity: The Meaning and Control of a Personal Death* (Springfield, Ill.: Chas. C. Thomas, 1974), p. 33.
13. Marya Mannes, *Last Rights: A Case for the Good Death* (New York: New American Library, 1973), p. 71.
14. Fred Cutter, *Coming to Terms with Death* (Chicago: Nelson-Hall, 1974), p. 181.
15. Stanley Keleman, *Living Your Dying* (New York: Random House, 1974), p. 147.
16. Krant, *Death and Dignity,* pp. 86–87.
17. Ibid., p. 64.
18. Leon R. Kass, "Averting One's Eyes or Facing the Music? On

Dignity and Death," in *Death Inside Out,* edited by Peter Steinfels and Robert Veatch (New York: Harper & Row, 1975), p. 106.

19. Davis W. Clark, *Death-Bed Scenes* (New York: Carlton and
Phillips, 1855), p. 330.

20. Raymond Moody, *Life after Life* (New York: Bantam Books,
1976), pp. 21ff.

CHAPTER EIGHT

1. See, for example, Kevin Ranaghan and Dorothy Ranaghan,
Catholic Pentecostals (Paramus, N.J.: Paulist Press, 1969).

2. Mircea Eliade, *Patterns in Comparative Religion* (Cleveland: World Publishing Co., 1967), p. 2.

3. Clifford Geertz, *The Interpretation of Cultures* (New York:
Basic Books, 1973), p. 90.

4. Ibid., pp. 93–94.

5. Ibid., p. 100. See also Mary Douglas, *Purity and Danger*
(Baltimore: Penguin Books, 1970).

6. Robert Bellah, "Civil Religion in America," in *Beyond Belief* (New York: Harper & Row, 1970).

7. Thomas Luckmann, *The Invisible Religion* (New York:
Macmillan, 1967).

8. Peter Berger, Brigitte Berger, and Hansfried Kellner, *The
Homeless Mind: Modernization and Consciousness* (New York:
Vintage Books, 1973), chapter 1.

9. See "The Harris Survey," *Current Opinion,* 4 (March 1976):
42.

10. Luckmann, *Invisible Religion,* p. 98.

11. Berger, Berger, and Kellner, *Homeless Mind,* chapter 10.

12. Luckmann, *Invisible Religion,* p. 98.

13. Ibid., p. 103.

14. Edwin Schur, *The Awareness Trap: Self-Absorption Instead of Social Change* (New York: McGraw-Hill, 1977); Russell
Jacoby, *Social Amnesia: A Critique of Contemporary Psychology
from Adler to Laing* (Boston: Beacon Press, 1975).

15. Luckmann, *Invisible Religion,* p. 97.

16. Jacoby, *Social Amnesia,* p. 68.

17. Jean Houston, at a conference on "Human Energy and Formation of the Future," New York City, November 1975.

18. Peter Marin, "The New Narcissism," *Harper's Magazine*
(October 1975); Christopher Lasch, "The Narcissist Society,"
New York Review of Books (September 30, 1976).

19. Marin, "The New Narcissism," p. 56.
20. Schur, *Awareness Trap.*
21. Luckmann, *Invisible Religion,* p. 115.

CHAPTER NINE

1. Rudolph Bultmann, "New Testament and Mythology," *Kerygma and Myth,* edited by Hans Werner Bartsch (New York: Harper and Row, 1961).
2. Reginald W. Bibby, "Why Conservative Churches Are *Really* Growing," *Journal for the Scientific Study of Religion* 17 (June, 1978) 129–37.: This essay is in response to Dean M. Kelley's *Why Conservative Churches Are Growing* (New York: Harper and Row, 1972).
3. See Paul Vitz, *Psychology as Religion: The Cult of Self-Worship* (Grand Rapids, Mich.: Wm. B. Eerdmans, 1977) for an extremely strong denunciation of psychological religiousness in the name of authentic Christianity.
4. C. G. Jung, *Aion: Researches into the Phenomenology of the Self, CW* 9_2 (Princeton, N.J.: Princeton University Press, 1970), pp. 36 ff.
5. Abraham Maslow, *Religions, Values, and Peak-Experiences* (New York: Viking Press, 1970), p. 28.
6. Jack Downing and Robert Marmorstein, *Dreams and Nightmares* (New York: Harper and Row, 1973), p. 139.
7. Martin Shepard, *Beyond Sex Therapy: A Manual for Discovering Personal Pleasure and Liberation* (New York: Penthouse Press, 1975), p. 14.
8. See, among others, Ludwig Wittgenstein, *Philosophical Investigations* (New York: Macmillan, 1953) and Hans Georg Gadamer, *Truth and Method* (New York: Seabury Press, 1975).
9. Gerhard Ebeling, *Introduction to a Theology of Language* (Philadelphia: Fortress Press, 1973), p. 203.
10. Kurt Back, *Beyond Words* (Baltimore: Penguin Books, 1973), p. 80.
11. June Regush and Nicholas Regush, *Dream Worlds* (New York: New American Library, 1977), p. 156.
12. Lawrence LeShan, *The Medium, the Mystic and the Physicist* (New York: Ballantine Books, 1975), pp. 61ff.
13. Maslow, *Religions,* p. 45.
14. Mircea Eliade, *Patterns in Comparative Religion* (Cleveland: World Publishing Co., 1967), p. 2.

15. Jean Houston, "Putting the First Man on Earth," *Saturday Review* (Feb. 22, 1975), p. 28.

16. Eliade, *Patterns* and *Cosmos and History* (New York: Harper and Row, 1959).

17. Paul Tillich, *The Courage to Be* (New Haven: Yale University Press, 1952), p. 32 ff.

Bibliography

Ariès, P. *Western Attitudes Toward Death.* Baltimore: Johns Hopkins University Press, 1974.

Assagioli, R. *Psychosynthesis.* New York: Viking, 1971.

Back, K. *Beyond Words.* Baltimore: Penguin, 1973.

Barnes, M., and Berke, J. *Two Accounts of a Journey Through Madness.* New York: Ballantine Books, 1973.

Bellah, R. "Civil Religion in America" in *Beyond Belief.* New York: Harper & Row, 1970.

Bengis, I. *Combat in the Erogenous Zone.* New York: Alfred A. Knopf, 1972.

Beradt, C. *The Third Reich of Dreams.* Chicago: Quadrangle, 1966.

Berger, P. *The Sacred Canopy.* Garden City, N.Y.: Anchor, 1969.

———, Berger, P. and Kellner, H. *The Homeless Mind: Modernization and Consciousness.* New York: Vintage Books, 1973.

———, and Luckmann, T. *The Social Construction of Reality: A Treatise in the Sociology of Knowledge.* Garden City, N.Y.: Anchor, 1967.

Bibby, R.W. "Why Conservative Churches Are *Really* Growing." *Journal for the Scientific Study of Religion* 17 (June, 1978): 129–37.

Boisen, A. *Out of the Depths.* New York: Harper, 1960.

——— *The Exploration of the Inner World.* Philadelphia: University of Pennsylvania Press, 1971.

Boston Women's Health Book Collective. *Our Bodies, Our Selves.*
New York: Simon and Schuster, 1973.

Bultmann, R. "New Testament and Mythology" in *Kerygma and
Myth,* edited by H.W. Bartsch. New York: Harper and Row,
1961.

Calvin, J. *Institutes of the Christian Religion,* edited by J.T.
McNeill. Philadelphia: Westminster Press, 1960.

Clark, D.W. *Death-Bed Scenes.* New York: Carlton and Phillips,
1855.

Comfort, A. *The Joy of Sex: A Gourmet Guide to Love Making.*
New York: Crown, 1972.

Crampton, M. "The Use of Mental Imagery in Psychosynthesis."
New York: Psychosynthesis Research Foundation, 1970.

Crisp, T. *Do You Dream?* New York: E.P. Dutton, 1972.

Cutter, F. *Coming to Terms with Death.* Chicago: Nelson-Hall,
1974.

Deikman, A.J. "Deautomatization and the Mystic Experience" in
Altered States of Consciousness, edited by C.T. Tart. Garden
City, N.Y.: Anchor, 1972.

Dodson, B. *Liberating Masturbation: a Meditation on Self-Love.*
New York: Bodysex Designs, 1974.

Donahue, J. J. *Dream Reality.* Oakland, Cal.: Bench Press, 1974.

Douglas, M. *Purity and Danger.* Baltimore: Penguin Books, 1970.

Downing, J., and Marmorstein, R. *Dreams and Nightmares.* New
York: Harper and Row, 1973.

Ebeling, G. *Introduction to a Theology of Language.* Philadelphia: Fortress Press, 1973.

Eliade, M. *Patterns in Comparative Religion.* Cleveland: World,
1967.

───── *Cosmos and History.* New York: Harper and Row, 1959.

Ellis, H. *The World of Dreams.* Boston: Houghton Mifflin, 1925.

Faraday, A. *The Dream Game.* New York: Harper and Row, 1974.

Fisher, S. *Understanding the Female Orgasm.* New York: Bantam Books, 1973.

Freud, S. *The Interpretation of Dreams.* New York: Avon, 1966.

Friday, N. *My Secret Garden: Women's Sexual Fantasies.* New
York: Pocket Books. 1974.

Friedrich, O. *Going Crazy: An Inquiry into Madness in Our
Time.* New York: Simon and Schuster, 1976.

Gadamer, H.G. *Truth and Method.* New York: Seabury Press,
1975.

Garfield, P. *Creative Dreaming.* New York: Ballantine, 1976.

Geertz, C. *The Interpretation of Cultures.* New York: Basic
Books, 1973.

Gotkin, J., and Gotkin, P. *Too Much Anger, Too Many Tears: A Personal Triumph Over Psychiatry.* New York: Quadrangle, 1975.

Greeley, A. *Ecstasy: A Way of Knowing.* Englewood Cliffs, N.J.: Prentice-Hall, 1974.

Green, H. *I Never Promised You a Rose Garden.* New York: New American Library, 1964.

Grof, S. *Realms of the Human Unconscious.* New York: Viking, 1975.

————, and Halifax, J. *The Human Encounter with Death.* New York: E.P. Dutton, 1977.

Hall, C.S., and Nordby, V.J. *The Individual and His Dreams.* New York: New American Library, 1972.

Hennell, T. *The Witnesses.* New Hyde Park, N.Y.: University Books, 1967.

Hillman, J. *Re-Visioning Psychology.* New York: Harper and Row, 1975.

Hite, S. *The Hite Report: A Nationwide Study of Female Sexuality.* New York: Dell, 1976.

Houston, J. "Putting the First Man on Earth." *Saturday Review* 204 (Feb. 22, 1975).

Jacoby, R. *Social Amnesia: A Critique of Contemporary Psychology from Adler to Laing.* Boston: Beacon Press, 1975.

James, W. *The Varieties of Religious Experience.* New York: Collier Books, 1968.

Jefferson, L. *These Are My Sisters.* Garden City, N.Y.: Anchor, 1974.

Julian of Norwich. *Showings.* New York: Paulist Press, 1978.

Jung, C.G. "On the Nature of Dreams" in *The Structure and Dynamics of the Psyche. (C.W.* 8) Princeton: Princeton University Press, 1972.

————. *Aion: Researches into the Phenomenology of the Self.* (*C.W.* 9₂) Princeton: Princeton University Press, 1970.

————. *Psychology and Alchemy. (C.W.* 12) Princeton: Princeton University Press, 1970.

Kass, L.R. "Averting One's Eyes or Facing the Music? On Dignity and Death" in *Death Inside Out,* edited by P. Steinfels, and R. Veatch. New York: Harper and Row, 1975.

Katz, J. *Dreams Are Your Truest Friends.* New York: Pocket Books, 1976.

Keleman, S. *Living Your Dying.* New York: Random House, 1974.

Kelley, D. *Why Conservative Churches Are Growing.* New York: Harper and Row, 1972.

Kline-Graber, G., and Graber, B. *Woman's Orgasm: A Guide to Sexual Satisfaction.* Indianapolis: Bobbs-Merrill, 1975.
Klinger, E. *The Structure and Functions of Fantasy.* New York: Wiley Interscience, 1971.
Krant, M.J. *Dying and Dignity: The Meaning and Control of a Personal Death.* Springfield, Ill.: Chas. C. Thomas, 1974.
Kübler-Ross, E. *On Death and Dying.* New York: Macmillan, 1969.
————, ed. *Death: The Final Stage of Growth.* Englewood Cliffs, N.J.: Prentice-Hall, 1975.
Laing, R.D. *The Politics of Experience.* New York: Ballantine Books, 1967.
Langone, J. *Vital Signs: The Way We Die in America.* Boston: Little, Brown and Co., 1974.
Larsen, S. *The Shaman's Doorway.* New York: Harper and Row, 1976.
Lasch, C. "The Narcissist Society." *New York Review of Books* (Sept. 30, 1976), p. 15.
LeShan, L. *The Medium, the Mystic, and the Physicist.* New York: Ballantine Books, 1975.
Leuba, J.H. *The Psychology of Religious Mysticism.* London: Routledge and Kegan Paul, 1972. First published 1925.
Lilly, J. *The Center of the Cyclone.* New York: Bantam Books, 1973.
Luckmann, T. *The Invisible Religion.* New York: Macmillan, 1967.
McCoy, M.C. *To Die with Style.* Nashville: Abingdon Press, 1974.
McLeester, D. *Welcome to the Magic Theater: A Handbook for Exploring Dreams.* Amherst, Mass.: Food for Thought Publications, 1977.
McLoughlin, W.G., ed. *The American Evangelicals, 1800–1900.* New York: Harper and Row, 1968.
Mannes, M. *Last Rights: A Case for the Good Death.* New York: New American Library, 1973.
Marin, P. "The New Narcissism." *Harper's Magazine* (Oct. 1975).
Maslow, A. *Toward a Psychology of Being.* Princeton, N.J.: D. Van Nostrand Co., 1968.
————. *Religions, Values and Peak-Experiences.* New York: Viking, 1970.
Masters, R.E.L., and Houston, J. *The Varieties of Psychedelic Experience.* New York: Dell, 1966.
Masters, W.H., and Johnson, V.E. *Human Sexual Response.* Boston: Little, Brown, 1966.
————. *The Pleasure Bond.* New York: Bantam Books, 1976.

Moody, R. *Life After Life.* New York: Bantam Books, 1976.
Morgan, M. *The Total Woman.* New York: Pocket Books, 1975.
Murray, H.A. "Techniques for a Systematic Investigation of Fantasy." *The Journal of Psychology* 3 (1936): 115–43.
Naranjo, C. *The One Quest.* New York: Ballantine Books, 1972.
Neary, J. *Whom the Gods Destroy.* New York: Atheneum, 1975.
O'Brien, B. *Operators and Things: The Inner Life of a Schizophrenic.* New York: New American Library, 1976.
Otto, R. *The Idea of the Holy.* London: Oxford University Press, 1976.
Pahnke, W.N., and Richards, W. "Implications of LSD and Experimental Mysticism" in *Altered States of Consciousness,* edited by C.T. Tart. Garden City, N.Y.: Anchor, 1972.
Perry, J.W. *The Roots of Renewal in Myth and Madness.* San Francisco: Jossey-Bass, 1976.
Proudfoot, W., and Shaver, P. "Attribution Theory and the Psychology of Religion" *Journal for the Scientific Study of Religion* 14 (Dec. 1975): 317–30.
Ranaghan, K., and Ranaghan, D. *Catholic Pentecostals.* Paramus, N.J.: Paulist Press, 1969.
Regush, June V. and Regush, Nicholas M. *Dream Worlds: The Complete Guide to Dreams and Dreaming.* New York: New American Library, 1977.
Riffel, H.H. *A Living, Loving Way.* Minneapolis: Bethany Fellowship, 1973.
Rosenham, D.L. "On Being Sane in Insane Places." *Science* 179 (Jan. 19, 1973): 250–58.
Roszak, T. *Where the Wasteland Ends.* Garden City, N.Y.: Doubleday, 1972.
Samuels, M., and Samuels, N. *Seeing with the Mind's Eye.* New York: Random House, 1975.
Scholem, G. *On the Kabbalah and Its Symbolism.* New York: Schocken Books, 1969.
Schulz, R., and Aderman, D. "Clinical Research and the Stages of Dying." *Omega* 5 (Summer, 1974): 137–44.
Schur, E. *The Awareness Trap: Self-Absorption Instead of Social Change.* New York: McGraw-Hill, 1977.
Seaman, B. *Free and Female.* Greenwich, Conn.: Fawcett Publications, 1972.
Sechrist, E. *Dreams, Your Magic Mirror.* New York: Warner Paperback Library, 1974.
Shepard, M. *Beyond Sex Therapy: A Manual for Discovering Personal Pleasure and Liberation.* New York: Penthouse Press, 1975.

186

BIBLIOGRAPHY

Sherfey, M. *The Nature and Evolution of Female Sexuality.* New York: Vintage, 1973.

Silverman, J. "Shamans and Acute Schizophrenia." *American Anthropologist* 69 (1967): 2–31.

Singer, J. *Daydreaming: An Introduction to the Experimental Study of Inner Experience.* New York: Random House, 1966.

———. *The Inner World of Daydreaming.* New York: Harper and Row, 1975.

Stace, W.I. *Mysticism and Philosophy.* Philadelphia: J.B. Lippincott, 1960.

Stewart, K. "Dream Theory in Malaya." in *Altered States of Consciousness,* edited by C.T. Tart. Garden City, N.Y.: Anchor, 1972.

Tart, C.T., ed. *Altered States of Consciousness.* Garden City, N.Y.: Anchor, 1972.

———, ed. *Transpersonal Psychologies.* New York: Harper and Row, 1975.

Teresa of Avila. *The Interior Castle.* New York: Doubleday, 1972.

———. *The Life of Teresa of Jesus.* Garden City, N.Y.: Image Books, 1960.

Thurber, J. "The Secret Life of Walter Mitty." *The Thurber Carnival.* New York: Harper and Row, 1975.

Tillich, P. *The Courage to Be.* New Haven: Yale University Press, 1952.

Tolstoy, L. *The Death of Ivan Ilyich and Other Stories.* New York: New American Library, 1960.

Underhill, E. *Mysticism.* New York: World Publishing, 1972.

Vitz, P. *Psychology as Religion: The Cult of Self-Worship.* Grand Rapids, Mich.: Wm. B. Eerdmans, 1977.

Vonnegut, M. *The Eden Express.* New York: Bantam Books. 1976.

Warren, J. *How to Be an Erotic Woman.* New York: Award Books, 1971.

Watkins, M. *Waking Dreams.* New York: Harper and Row, 1976.

Weber, M. *The Protestant Ethic and the Spirit of Capitalism.* New York: Scribners, 1958.

Weisman, A.D. *On Dying and Denying.* New York: Behavioral Publications, 1972.

White, J., ed. *The Highest State of Consciousness.* Garden City, N.Y.: Anchor, 1972.

Wittgenstein, L. *Philosophical Investigations.* New York: Macmillan, 1953.

Wolfe, K.K., and Wolfe, G.K. "Metaphors of Madness: Popular Psychological Narratives." *Journal of Popular Culture* 4 (Spring, 1976).

Index

Thurber, James, 39
Tillich, Paul, 160, 167
Tinkering attitude: body and, 88;
   dreams and, 22; dying and, 108;
   in modern society, 131–32; sexuality and, 90; True Self and, 162
To Die with Style, 103
Tolstoy, Count Leo, 111
*Too Much Anger, Too Many
   Tears,* 76
Tradition, 1, 8, 151, 152; identity
   and, 133; inner experience vs.,
   129–30, 150–51; rejected, 4,
   150–52
Transcendental experience, 69,
   82–83. *See also* Mystical experi-
   ence; Peak-experience
Transformation. *See* Change
True Self, 29, 81; as hierophany,
   21, 141–42, 160–64; narcissism
   and, 141–42; as source of
   dreams, 20–21
*Two Accounts of a Journey
   Through Madness,* 76

Unconscious: Freud's view of, 19;
   Jung's view of, 19; trust in, 21,
   49
Union, sense of, 52–53, 57, 60, 65,
   90, 102
Universalism, 106, 115, 166; mystical experience and, 52, 53, 55,
   61
Upanishads, 141

Vagina and vaginal orgasm, 91,
   94
Values: Being-values, 58, 120; of
   inner experience advocates, 3,

5, 20–22, 24–27, 29–30, 41, 43, 81,
   96, 105–6, 113–15, 120, 139–41, 150;
   sexuality and, 92–100; in study
   of religion, ix; in sociology,
   132
Victimization: feelings of, 25, 28,
   30, 114, 138–39; and mental patients, 70, 80
"The Vision of the World Clock,"
   46
Visions: Jungian view of, 46–47;
   mystical experience and, 64–65;
   religious, 45
Vonnegut, Mark, 75, 76, 84

Waking fantasy, 45–47. *See also*
   Daydream
Waking life: dreams and, 16, 23,
   28–30; victimization and, 28. *See
   also* Day-world/night-world
   split
Warren, Joy, 99
Weber, Max, 35
"We-situation," 96, 141
Western culture: dreams and, 13;
   as hostile to inner experience,
   8; sexuality and, 88
Women: body and, 88, 98–99; ca-
   pacity for orgasm, 91; power
   and, 96, 99; self-affirmation and,
   97–98; as sex-objects, 99; sexual
   fantasies and, 42–43
Word, in Western religion, 153
Words. *See* Language
World view, 128–30; modern
   American, 130, 155

Zen, 163